International Migration.
A Quick Immersion

Quick Immersions provide illuminating introductions to diverse topics in the worlds of social science, the hard sciences, philosophy and the humanities. Written in clear and straightforward language by prestigious authors, the texts also offer valuable insights to readers seeking a deeper knowledge of those fields.

Elżbieta M. Goździak

INTERNATIONAL MIGRATION
A Quick Immersion

Tibidabo Publishing
New York

Published by Tibidabo Publishing, Inc. New York.

Copyediting by Lori Gerson
Cover art by Raimon Guirado

First published 2021

Visit our Series on our Web:
www.quickimmersions.com

ISBN: 978-1-949845-27-3
1 2 3 4 5 6 7 8 9 10

Library of Congress Control Number: 2021935891

Printed in the United States of America.

Contents

Introduction: Writing about Migration
during a Pandemic   7

1. Why Migration Matters   12
2. Scope of International Migration   38
3. Types of Migrants   46
4. Nations of Immigrants: the United States, Canada,
   and Australia   62
5. Europe: A Continent on the Move   94
6. The Immigrant Experience: Focus on Integration   102
7. Diasporas and Transnational Communities   117
8. Securitization of Migration   133
Future Challenges   139
Further Reading   148

Introduction:
Writing about Migration during a Pandemic

It seems a bit surreal to write a book about international migration during a pandemic. COVID-19 brought human mobility to a screeching halt. Before the pandemic, it was estimated that more than a million people were literally flying through the air at any given moment. Currently, 91 percent of the world's population live in countries with coronavirus restrictions on foreign arrivals. Gillian Triggs of the United Nations High Commissioner for Refugees (UNHCR) recently told the *New York Times* that, for all intents and purposes, refugee resettlement has stopped as only 30 of more than 120 countries that have closed their borders are giving any consideration to the claims of asylum seekers.

After 9/11, the Federal Aviation Administration (FAA) shutdown airspace across the United States, and within just a few hours almost all aircrafts were grounded. The same is happening now, but on a global scale. It is an unprecedented global cessation of movement in modern times. While many people compare COVID-19 to the 1918 'Spanish flu' pandemic, in terms of migration the situation in 1918 was markedly different than it is now, in 2020.

The influenza pandemic of 1918–1919 coincided with a major wave of immigration to the United States. Between 1880 and the 1920s, some 23.5 million newcomers from Southern and Eastern Europe, Asia, Canada, and Mexico arrived in the United States. The immigrants needed information and assistance in coping with the influenza. As Alan Kraut, a Canadian migration scholar, reminds us, immigrant physicians, community spokespeople, newspapers, and religious and fraternal groups, members of the two largest groups of immigrants, Southern Italians and Eastern European Jews, shouldered the burden. They disseminated public health information in culturally sensitive manners and in languages the newcomers understood, offering crucial services both to immigrants and American public health officials.

In 2020, the United States was closed to new immigrants and refugees. As of mid-July, 2020, with fewer than three months of the fiscal year left, only 7,848 refugees had been admitted for resettlement. Since the start of the COVID-19 pandemic, the Trump

Administration has issued at least 48 policy changes affecting almost every facet of the immigration system. While some of these policies are reasonable changes, their duration is indefinite, allowing restrictions to potentially remain in place long after the pandemic. The Biden administration is moving to reverse many of the restrictions Trump instituted, but COVID-19 is not necessarily cooperating with Biden's desire to reopen the country to immigrants and refugees.

The question is whether COVID-19 lockdown represents a temporary trough in global population movements or whether we are witnessing the end of the most recent age of migration. Alan Gamlen, a human geographer at Monash University in Australia, suggests that high rates of unemployment might adversely affect labor migration as countries will feel political pressure to hire native workers. The political pressure might be there, but will native workers be available and willing to take low-paying jobs? Being on lockdown since mid-March, 2020 when I returned from Europe to Washington, D.C., I continue to rely on grocery and medication deliveries. Virtually every person that brings the necessities to my doorstep is an immigrant. With walls going up across Europe, migrant labor from the East became crucial to food security and international supply chains. Lockdowns across Europe have revealed an acute shortage of agricultural workers. Farmers in the United Kingdom, Germany, and France worry that the workers they recruit domestically will lack the skills necessary to efficiently harvest crops without damaging them. Agribusinesses across Western Europe chartered flights to bring hundreds of Eastern Europeans to work the fields.

I am optimistic that the pandemic will be over once a vaccine is widely available. While I do not think we will necessarily return to what we considered 'normal' before COVID-19, I hope people will again be able to exercise their fundamental human right to migrate.

We might be able to defeat COVID, but will we be able to conquer anti-immigrant sentiments that have been on the rise across the globe for some time? Citizens are concerned about the failure of politicians to show effective leadership on migration. Ill-informed understanding of migration—and resulting xenophobia and racism against refugees and immigrants—has people turning to populist politicians who wish to bring back protectionism, reverse globalization, and erect walls and fences. In this short book, I want to dispel some of the misperceptions that migrants are the source of societal ills and provide non-specialists with a basic understanding of the phenomenon of international migration to be able to engage in constructive debates on refugees and migrants around dinner tables and in public spaces.

I cannot possibly discuss all aspects of international migration. Therefore, I decided to write about the issues that interest me both as a migration scholar and a migrant myself. I chose topics that I have done research on during my long career as a scholar of international migration. I begin this book with an attempt to answer the question why migration matters and why it is important to have a basic knowledge of international migration issues. I write about the contributions immigrants have made in every corner of the world where they settled. At the same time, I also discuss the ill effects of the early European settlers on indigenous people. I move on to discuss different types of migration and different categories of migrants, fully cognizant of the fact that legal definitions do not always match the myriad identities migrants express. I provide a glimpse of the three countries—Australia, Canada, and the United States—that are quintessential countries of immigration. I go on to discuss mobility and migration within Europe. I follow with some reflections on immigrant integration. Since immigrants no longer sever ties with their countries of origin, but rather live transnational lives, both physically and in cyberspace, I look at the concepts of diaspora and transnationalism. Given the war on terror, I discuss securitization of international migration. I end with some thoughts on the challenges laying ahead.

Chapter 1

Why Migration Matters

Migration matters for many reasons. The current pandemic notwithstanding, human mobility has been an enduring feature of the global history. We would be hard pressed to talk about human development without reference to migration. Africa as the cradle of humanity is where people moved from and eventually spread around the globe. The human world as we know it today has been created through migration, starting with the initial migration of the early genus *Homo*, around two million years ago. Yes, you read it right, two million years!

Today, scientists believe that from their beginnings in Africa, modern humans went first to Asia between 80,000 and 60,000 years ago. By 45,000 years ago, they had settled Indonesia, Papua New Guinea, and Australia. The moderns entered Europe around 40,000 years ago, probably via two routes: from Turkey along the Danube corridor into eastern Europe, and along the Mediterranean coast. By 35,000 years ago, they were firmly established in most of the Old World. The Neanderthals, forced into mountain strongholds in Croatia, the Iberian Peninsula, the Crimea and elsewhere, would become extinct 25,000 years ago. Finally, around 15,000 years ago, humans crossed from Asia to North America and from there to South America. The prehistoric migrations of hunter-gatherers and agriculturalists formed the foundation for the ethnic and linguistic patterns that spanned the globe before 1500 CE. Many more migrations followed. The five volumes of *The Encyclopedia of Global Human Migration*, edited by Immanuel Ness, with contributions from hundreds of scholars, give us a glimpse at the scale and importance of migration to human history.

Depending on where we live, particular population movements come to mind as the most important or most memorable or the largest. As a migration scholar and an immigrant from Poland to the United States, I am partial to immigration from Europe to the United States at the end of the nineteenth and beginning of the twentieth centuries.

Granted, immigrants started coming to the U.S. much earlier. During the colonial period some 400,000 English came to America. However, the immigration of Europeans at the beginning of the 1900s gave birth to migration theories and migration scholarship. While many of these theories no longer fit the globalized world we live in, equally many are used to understand contemporary population mobility. The peak year of European immigration was in 1907, when 1,285,349 persons entered the country. The research on these immigrants, especially studies undertaken by the Chicago school sociologists--George Herbert Mead, Robert E. Park, W. I. Thomas, and Florian Znaniecki-- set the course for migration studies for decades to come. Contemporary migration scholars might have rejected the assimilationist theories, but policy-makers, even those who talk about integration of immigrants into host societies, continue to operationalize these new concepts as assimilation or the processes of turning 'them' into 'us.' I will return to the issue of integration later in this book.

Let's turn to two other population movements important in relation to migration to and within the United States, namely forced migration of African slaves and the Great Migration of African Americans from the rural South to the cities of the North, Midwest, and West. Some 12 million African slaves were brought forcibly to the Americas between the 1500s and the 1860s. This largest forced migration in human history relocated some 50 ethnic and linguistic groups. Only a small portion of the enslaved—about half a million -- went to North America; the majority went to South America and the Caribbean.

The Great Migration saw six million African Americans leave the South between 1916 and 1930 and from 1940 to 1970. Racial discrimination and violence propagated by oppressive Jim Crow laws as well as poverty and lack of employment opportunities were the major reasons for leaving the South. The Boll Weevil infestation destroyed the cotton industry between 1915 and 1920 and deprived many African Americans of livelihoods, but employment opportunities were the factor that drew them North where World War I created jobs in factories and on railroads.

In his *Migration Series*, Jacob Lawrence, an African American artist, tells the story of the mass movement of African Americans from the rural South to major industrial centers of the North, particularly Chicago, Detroit, Cleveland, St. Louis, Pittsburgh, Philadelphia, and New York City, better than any migration scholar could. Following the example of *griot*, the West African storyteller, who spins tales of the past that have meaning for the present and the future, Lawrence masterfully told a story that reminds us of history and invites us to reflect on the universal theme of struggle in the world today: "To me, migration means movement. There was conflict and struggle. But out of the struggle came a kind of power and even beauty. 'And the migrants kept coming' is a refrain of triumph over adversity. If it rings true for you today, then it must still strike a chord in our American experience," wrote Lawrence. Completing his series of 60 panels in 1941 at the start of the second Great Migration, Lawrence understood that the ongoing impact of this migration would continue to reverberate for decades to come.

The series was the subject of a solo show at the Downtown Gallery in Manhattan in 1941, making Lawrence one of the first black artists to be represented by a New York gallery. Interest in the series was enormous. Ultimately, The Phillips Collection and New York's Museum of Modern Art (MOMA) agreed to divide it, with the Phillips buying the odd-numbered and MOMA the even-numbered paintings. In 2016, the Phillips organized an exhibition of the whole series. It was a sight to behold.

The Great Migration of African Americans shows that migration does not necessarily involve crossing of international borders. One of the largest internal migrations involved rural to urban migration in China. The relaxation of migration rules following the death of Mao Zedong in 1976 and the poverty that has ravaged rural China have given immense impetus to rural-urban migration within China. Migrant workers have transformed the economy of China providing much needed cheap labor to fuel the export-led boom of the Chinese economy. Currently, migrant workers make up approximately 12 percent of the country's population. However, the Chinese government expects another 100 million people to move to cities by the end of 2020.

Intra- and intercontinental migration has been very important to post-colonial Africa. After independence, millions of Africans were forced to migrate internally and across borders of countries such as Algeria, Kenya, South Africa, and Southern Rhodesia (today part of Zimbabwe). Large numbers of Africans continue to move both within and from the continent. According to the International Organization for Migration (IOM), in 2019, over 21 million Africans were living in another African country, a significant increase from 2015, when an estimated 18.5 million Africans lived within the continent, but outside the country of their origin. The number of African migrants living outside the continent has more than doubled since 1990. Migration from Africa to Europe has been the largest. In 2019, 10.6 million Africans lived in Europe, 4.6 million resided in Asia, and 3.2 million in North America.

Although forced displacement is a global phenomenon, it is more pronounced in Africa. Numerous coups and presidential assassinations across the continent coupled with armed conflicts displaced millions of people. According to the UN High Commissioner for Refugees (UNHCR), Sub-Saharan Africa alone hosts more than 26 percent of the world's 20.4 million refugees. At the end of 2018, the continent hosted some 17.8 million internally displaced persons (IDPs). The African Union declared 2019 as *The Year of Refugees, Returnees and Internally Displaced Persons: Towards Durable Solutions to Forced Displacement.* Unfortunately, durable solutions have not been attained yet. The number of refugees and IDPs has soared in recent years due to ongoing crises in the Central African Republic, Nigeria, and South Sudan. New conflicts erupting in Burundi and Yemen have also contributed to the growing numbers of displaced persons.

If you live on the Indian subcontinent, you might first think about the 15 million people who found themselves stranded in the 'wrong' part of the land, Hindus in Pakistani territory and Muslims in Indian territory, following the partition of British India in 1947. After the partition, there began one of the greatest migrations in human history, as millions of Muslims trekked to West and East Pakistan (the latter now known as Bangladesh) while millions of Hindus and Sikhs headed in the opposite direction.

Emotions ran high and terrible atrocities were committed on both sides, ranging from damage to property, arson, killing, and mob violence. Ordinary peace-loving Hindus and Muslims became so enraged with each other that they committed atrocities they would never have considered themselves capable off. In some places, even state troops joined the violence. On August 9, 1947, a train carrying Muslim officers from Delhi to Karachi was intercepted and

150 officers were massacred. Soon trains of migrants began to arrive at their destination filled with dead bodies and their caravans intercepted and looted.

If your gaze falls on Southeast Asia, you might consider the migration stemming from the aftermath of the Vietnam War. After the fall of Saigon in 1975, the United States evacuated approximately 125,000 Vietnamese refugees in the first phase of the Vietnamese refugee resettlement. Over the next 25 years, more than three million people would undertake the dangerous journey to become refugees in other countries of Southeast Asia, Hong Kong, or China. According to the United Nations High Commissioner for Refugees (UNHCR), 250,000 Vietnamese refugees had perished at sea by July 1986. More than 2.5 million Indochinese were resettled, mostly in North America, Australia, and Europe. More than 525,000 were repatriated, either voluntarily or involuntarily, mainly to Cambodia.

I could provide many more examples, but the point here is that no continent has escaped the effects of out- or in-migration. Today, virtually all countries in the world are simultaneously countries of destination, origin, and transit for international migrants. With a record 258 million people living outside their country of birth, international migration is a global phenomenon with profound demographic, economic, social, and political implications for both sending and receiving countries. The scale of some of these movements defy our imagination, especially when we think about the times when mobility was much more limited and difficult, and journeys took a long time and required crossing oceans or vast territories of land without the aid of planes and fast trains.

Immigrants' contributions to their adopted countries

Migration matters because immigrants have made innumerable contributions to their adopted countries. Don't get me wrong, the potential of immigrants has not always been recognized. Two hundred years ago in the United States, Benjamin Franklin worried that German immigrants would swamp America's predominantly British culture. When the Irish immigrants arrived in America, they were disparaged as lazy drunks, not to mention Roman Catholics. When Poles, Italians, and Russian Jews arrived, many people were skeptical whether they would be able to integrate into American life. Today the same fears are raised about immigrants from Mexico, Latin America, Africa, and Asia, but current critics of immigration are as wrong as their counterparts were in previous eras.

Immigration has not undermined the American experiment. Immigrants and their children have contributed to performing arts, the movie industry, literature, sciences, political life, and many other fields. Immigrants to other countries made similar contributions.

The contribution of immigrants to twentieth century American popular music is well known. Irving Berlin's *White Christmas, Easter Parade, God Bless America* are household tunes in the United States and beyond. Some of the most highly regarded composers and playwrights of Broadway were children of immigrants, including George and Ira Gershwin, and Leonard Bernstein. First-generation Eastern European Jewish immigrants created the American movie industry. Frank Capra, born in Italy in 1897, came to the United States as a child and became one of the most celebrated American film-makers. He is best remembered for *Mr. Smith Goes to Washington* (1939) and *It's a Wonderful Life* (1947). Capra's movies helped reinforce beliefs in the American dream.

Connoisseurs of classical music know that Fryderyk Chopin was a child of a French immigrant to Poland. Given the politically unstable situation in Poland following the November 1830 uprising against Russian rule, Chopin went to Paris and became part of the Great Emigration (1831-1870) of thousands of Poles from the political and cultural élites. Many other musicians and composers left their native lands. Russian émigré Igor Stravinsky may be the best known of the European musicians who made Los Angeles his home. He spent three decades based in Los Angeles, where he developed a close collaboration with choreographer George Balanchine, another Russian immigrant.

E. Ce Miller wrote about the importance of immigrant writers to literature, especially now in times of nationalist rhetoric and growing xenophobia. It's critical, she said, to continue to listen to the voices of those who come from other places, foreign traditions, different religions, unfamiliar social and political structures, diverse ideologies and ways of living, and landscapes dissimilar from our own. In my opinion, books by immigrant writers are essential to the beauty and diversity of literature. They remind us, the readers, of both the differences and the commonalities of our lives. The list of immigrant writers is long. Some of my favorites include: Viet Thanh Nguyen, the Pulitzer Prize winner and author of *The Refugees* and *The Sympathizer*, among others; Kazuo Ishiguro, the recipient of the 2017 Nobel Prize in Literature; Moshin Hamid, whose book *Exit West* I assign in my class on Accented Narratives; Jhumpa Lahiri, author of *The Namesake* and *The Lowland*; Lisa Ko, author of *The Leavers*; and many, many more.

Immigrants make up 13 percent of the U.S. population, but American foreign-born scientists constitute more than a third of Nobel Prize winners in science and technology. Albert Einstein, perhaps the most famous scientist of all time, was a refugee. My fellow-compatriot, Maria Skłodowska-Curie, left her native Poland to study at the Sorbonne in Paris. She will forever be remembered as the first woman to win a Nobel Prize, the first person – and the only woman – to win twice, and the only person to win a Nobel Prize in two different sciences: physics and chemistry.

In my own discipline, anthropology, several of the most famous anthropologists were immigrants. Franz Boas (born in Germany), Arjun Appadurai (born in India), and Carlos Castaneda (born in Peru) immigrated to the United States, while Bronisław Malinowski (born in Poland) lived and worked in the United Kingdom.

Contemporary migrants, including undocumented immigrants and irregular migrants, have also made significant contributions to their adopted societies. For example, recipients of the Deferred Action for Childhood Arrivals (DACA) provisions bring in billions of dollars to the U.S. economy every year. Currently, DACA youth alone add an estimated $42 billion to the GDP every year.

Immigrants make up 17 percent of the U.S. labor force but pay the government billions in taxes. Contrary to popular assumptions, undocumented immigrants also contribute to the economy. Undocumented immigrants pay an estimated $11.6 billion a year in taxes, according to the Institute on Taxation & Economic Policy. In 2017, immigrants made up almost 30 percent of all new entrepreneurs in the United States. Immigrants continue to be nearly twice as likely as native-born people to start businesses. Tech giants and startups such as Amazon, Apple, Google, Yahoo, Microsoft, and Oracle, were founded and continue to be led by immigrants or their children. Nearly 44 percent of the companies on the 2018 Fortune 500 list were founded by immigrants or children of immigrants. Together, in fiscal year 2017, these companies brought in $5.5 trillion in revenue—a figure that is greater than the gross domestic product (GDP) of every country in the world other than the United States and China.

In many developing countries, the remittances migrants send home far exceed the aid provided by rich countries. According to the World Bank, remittance flows to low- and middle-income countries reached $551 billion in 2019, up by 4.7 percent compared to 2018. Before the pandemic the World Bank expected remittances to reach $597 billion by 2021. However, just as COVID-19 has disproportionately impacted some communities more than others, the virus has had a negative impact on migrant workers. Surprisingly, despite the bleak experience of labor migrants during the pandemic, its effect on remittances has, in many cases, proven resilient, claims the International Monetary Fund. But that trend may yet be upended.

The effects of migration on indigenous populations

Contributions to their adopted lands notwithstanding, arrival of early migrants had devastating effects on indigenous populations. Let's just pause for a moment and think about the impact of the arrival of white settlers on aboriginal populations in Australia, on First Nations in Canada, and on Native Americans in the United States.

Aboriginal Australians occupied the continent for more than 65,000 years before the arrival of English colonial settlers in 1788. Estimates regarding precontact population size of indigenous Australians vary widely. A. R. Radcliffe-Brown estimated that there were between 250,000 and 300,000 aborigines, while D.J. Mulvaney and J.P. White put the number at 700,000 people. Eleanor Bourke estimated that in 1788 between 300,000 and one million indigenous people inhabited Australia. However, by 1901 fewer than 100,000 of them remained. There were between 600 and 700 cultural-linguistic groups when English settlers arrived in Australia, but today only about 250 languages are in use.

If you watched the movie *Rabbit-Proof Fence*, directed and produced by Phillip Noyce and based on the 1996 book *Follow the Rabbit-Proof Fence* by Doris Pilkington Garimara, you are familiar with the brutal removals of children referred to as "half-caste" conducted between 1905 and 1967. Australia's Stolen Generations included children of Australian Aboriginals and Torres Strait Islanders who were forcibly removed from their families by the Australian federal and state government agencies and church missions, under acts of their respective parliaments. The effects of the family separations were devastating. In 2008, the Australian Prime Minister at the time, Kevin Rudd, formally apologized to the country's indigenous peoples, particularly to the Stolen Generations, whose lives had been blighted by past government policies of forced child removal and indigenous assimilation.

Residential schools were also part of the Canadian First Nations' history. They were religious schools, sponsored by the government, with the goal of assimilating indigenous children into Euro-Canadian culture. Most were established around 1880; the last residential school closed in 1996. Former students have demanded recognition and restitution, resulting in the Indian Residential Schools Settlement Agreement in 2007 and a formal public apology by Prime Minister Stephen Harper in 2008. In total, an estimated 150,000 First Nation, Inuit, and Métis children attended residential schools. In 2017, Prime Minister Justin Trudeau offered another, very emotional apology to indigenous people in the province of Newfoundland and Labrador, where for much of the twentieth century indigenous children were compelled to attend boarding schools that separated them from their families and cultures and, in many cases, subjected them to abuse. Newfoundland and Labrador did not join Canada until 1949. Its boarding school system had different origins even if it had a similar legacy. In

2008, Mr. Harper's government took the view that the abuses committed there in the early twentieth century were not the federal government's fault. A national Truth and Reconciliation Commission later condemned the boarding school system as a form of "cultural genocide."

Similar separation of children from their native families occurred in the United States. On March 3, 1819, the Civilization Fund Act ushered in an era of assimilationist policies, leading to the establishment of Indian boarding-schools that operated from 1860 to 1978. The act directly spurred the creation of the schools by putting forward the notion that native culture and language were to blame for what was deemed the country's "Indian problem." Mary Annette Pember wrote in *The Atlantic* about the effects of the legacy of boarding schools, created to destroy and vilify native culture, language, family, and spirituality, on her own family. Her mother, Bernice, was a survivor of Saint Mary's Catholic Indian Boarding School on the Ojibwe reservation in Odanah, Wisconsin. While the Australian and Canadian Prime Ministers personally apologized to the respective native communities, the US. apology to Native Americans took until 2009 and came stealthily tucked away in an unrelated spending bill. President Obama publicly acknowledged the "Apology to Native Peoples of the United States" in 2010. But Obama did more. Keeping his 2008 campaign promise, President Obama held eight

White House Tribal Nations Conferences, one every year he was in office. These conferences marked the first time in history that any American president has met with tribes on such a large scale and on a regular basis.

Under the Trump administration, children were separated from their families, but this time the children were immigrant children. The so-called "zero tolerance" policy, dictating that all migrants who cross the U.S. border without permission, including those seeking asylum, be referred to the Department of Justice for prosecution, ended in 2018 after nation-wide protest swept the country. However, prior to it ending, some 3,000 children under the age of 18 were handed over to the Office of Refugee Resettlement (ORR), which shipped them miles away from their parents and scattered them among 100 shelters and other care arrangements across the country. Hundreds of these children, including infants and toddlers, were under the age of five, many came from indigenous communities in Guatemala, Mexico, and Nicaragua. As I write this in the early fall of 2020, 666 children are still separated from their families. The government seems to be unable to find their parents.

Now all eyes are on President Biden and the task force he promised to establish to reunite separated families. The First Lady's chief of staff, former U.S. ambassador to Uruguay, Julissa Reynoso, will monitor the federal reunification effort.

Migration and politics

Today, migration is at the top of the political agenda, attracts sustained attention in the media, and divides public opinion like never before. Obviously, there have always been anti-immigrant sentiments and even legislation to exclude particular groups of people from coming and settling in certain countries.

In the United States, there was the Chinese Exclusion Act of 1882 that restricted immigration of Chinese people for many years. Chinese immigrants and their American-born families remained ineligible for citizenship until 1943. American experience with Chinese exclusion spurred later movements for immigration restriction against other 'undesirable' groups such as Middle Easterners, Hindu, and East Indians, and the Japanese with the passage of the Immigration Act of 1924.

In the nineteenth century, immigration to Canada was largely unrestricted. This mostly 'open door' policy encouraged white immigration to Canada. However, Canada was not open to all. The first Immigration Act, which passed in 1869, specifically discriminated against immigrants on the grounds of class and disability. Later on, immigrants were discriminated on the basis of race. In 1885, under pressure from British Columbia, the federal government restricted Chinese immigration, first by imposing a head tax and later by passing the Chinese Immigration Act of 1923. These explicitly racist measures directed at the Chinese continued until the late 1940s.

Europe is often called Fortress Europe, because immigration to many European countries has been difficult. However, no European country has ever passed legislation similar to the U.S. Chinese Exclusion Act or the Canadian Chinese Immigration Act. Nonetheless, several European countries attempted to curtail immigration in the 1970s. Ultimately these efforts were unsuccessful in part because of court reversals of attempts to restrict family unification. Moreover, in the long run these decisions resulted in the development of an impressive range of immigrant rights. France, for example, made a decision in September 1977 to suspend family unification for three years. The following year, this decision was reversed by the Council of State and set the stage for continuing immigration. The German Federal Constitutional Court made similar decisions in 1973 ('The Arab Case'), 1978 ('The Indian Case'), and 1988 ('The Turkish and Yugoslav Cases'), but in 1990, Germany passed the long-debated Foreigners Act. The legislation codified most of the stipulations of the preceding court decisions. The unintended consequence of these decisions was a transformation of labor migration, often temporary, into family migration with permanent settlement.

Refugee crisis

Currently, migration debates, especially in Europe, focus on the 'refugee crisis.' But is it a crisis? What kind of a crisis? It certainly does not seem to be a *refugee* crisis, because the people fleeing armed conflicts and prosecution are not the problem. Catherine Woollard, the Secretary General of the European Council on Refugees and Exiles (ECRE), posits that what is often called 'the refugee crisis' is in fact a deep European political crisis which unfolded in 2015/2016, paralyzing decision-making and creating deep, probably irreparable, divisions between EU Member States.

Undeniably, large numbers of asylum seekers and migrants reached Europe in recent years. The highest number of arrivals - 1,015,078 - was recorded in 2015. More than 800,000 migrants were smuggled by sea from Turkey to Greece, and the majority continued to travel through Europe to reach Germany and Sweden. These are indeed sizable populations of asylum seekers, but do they constitute a 'crisis'? Today's exodus from the Middle East pales in comparison with the situation Germany faced, and surmounted, after World War II. At the end of WWII, there were some 11 million displaced people in Germany alone. They were slave laborers, prisoners of war, and Holocaust survivors. The Germans who had lived in Eastern Europe were being expelled from Czechoslovakia, Poland, and Hungary. The arrival of several million newcomers in Europe in recent years presents real challenges, of course, but a prosperous European Union with a population in excess of 500 million has the means to overcome them, doesn't it?

'Crisis,' a concept which the Greeks used to delineate stark alternatives—right or wrong, salvation or damnation, life or death—has constantly framed modern ideas of history. Migration scholars, however, argue that face-value acceptance of crisis narratives related to recent arrivals of asylum seekers in Europe results in viewing and managing migration according to binary divisions: integration versus segregation, modernity versus cultural backwardness, the deserving versus the undeserving, and through the manufactured dichotomy between refugees and economic migrants.

Cautionary lectures by migration scholars notwithstanding, politicians have certainly been exploiting the powerful narrative of 'crisis' as a political tactic. Sebastian Kurz, the Federal Chancellor of Austria and a rising star of Europe's center right, in an article published in *Time* magazine in 2017, invoked 'crisis' multiple times. He paired the term with phrases such as 'loss of control,' 'overwhelmed by developments,' 'a huge challenge for our country,' 'regain control,' and 'find solutions.' Viktor Orbán, the Prime Minister of Hungary, has exploited the crisis narrative to defend his draconian measures aimed not only at barring refugees from Hungary, but also at criminalizing assistance to refugees and migrants. When some 400,000, mainly Muslim, refugees and asylum-seekers crossed the Serbian-Hungarian border and descended on the Keleti Railway Station in Budapest in 2015, Viktor Orbán did not see the refugees fleeing war-torn countries as a humanitarian challenge but as a Muslim invasion that required an appropriate response: closing the Balkan land route to the European Union and pressing the 'moral panic button.' His friend, Jarosław Kaczyński, the president of the Law and Justice (PiS) party in Poland, has also been making the most of the crisis narrative despite the fact that, with the exception of some Chechens, there are virtually no refugees in Poland.

Us and Them?

The crisis narrative fuels the distinction between Us and Them, citizens and migrants. Considered incompatible with 'European values,' religious beliefs, cultural expressions of faith exhibited by Muslim refugees are construed as a threat to the Christian identity of Europe. The perceived incompatibility of Christian and Muslim values allegedly makes Muslim refugees and migrants unable to integrate into the wider European societies and become Us.

I wonder whether the strong focus on shared 'European values' is as essential to immigrant integration as policy-makers in Brussels, Paris, Budapest, Warsaw, and elsewhere believe. The term

'European values' has been contested by many. Even before the expansion of the European Union (EU) into Central and Eastern Europe in 2004, scholars have deliberated who and what counts as 'European.' A familiar binary – the making of the 'European' Self and the casting out of a 'non-European' Other is at the heart of such identity formation. With increased migration, these debates have intensified despite the fact that Europe has always been a diverse continent in which Christian, Muslim, Jewish, and secular traditions have been present for centuries. The diversity of these traditions is what makes the cosmopolitan Europe vibrant and worth preserving, doesn't it?

Moreover, presenting shared 'European values' as bright ideals while failing to acknowledge violations of rights in the host society is not acceptable. Additionally, many of the values presented as 'European values' are in fact liberal democratic values. Care needs to be taken not to conflate the two; otherwise, we are talking about a top-down imposition of 'elite' values biased towards social and cultural norms of the majority. The challenge European policy-makers face is how to define values in non-ethnic, non-religious, and inclusive ways to signal to refugees and immigrants from day one that they are part of 'us' and an important element in ensuring social cohesion in Europe. Values based on ethno-cultural practices do not lead to positive integration outcomes in diverse societies. There is a need to engage newcomers in a thoughtful dialogue to identify what values they want to impart on their children as the second generation grows up in Europe. We might be pleasantly surprised how many values we share and how much we all have in common.

The aging of societies and migration

Migration matters to the demographics of the world. Europeans are living longer and healthier lives. However, this spectacular achievement is accompanied by fertility rates below replacement levels. As a result, population growth is slowing down while population ageing accelerates. Eurostat projects that by 2050 the proportion of people aged 65 and over will exceed 30 percent in Germany, all of Southern Europe, and most of Eastern Europe. Demographic ageing is already pervasive in Italy and Germany, where some 20 percent of the population is over 65 years of age, and other EU countries follow closely. Ireland is the main exception with only 12 percent of its population aged 65+.

The graying of America will also be inescapable in fewer than two decades, says the U.S. Census Bureau. Older adults are projected to outnumber kids for the first time in U.S. history. The middle-aged already outnumber children, but the country will reach a new milestone in 2034 when older adults will edge out children in population size. People age 65 and over are expected to number 77.0 million, while children under age 18 will number 76.5 million.

Population ageing presents serious challenges to many Western nations, particularly with respect to the care needed for a growing number of older people. Alessio Cangiano argues that the significant growth of the care workforce that will be required to meet the future needs of Europe's ageing population is unlikely to be achieved by relying exclusively on domestic labor supply. The EU is projecting a shortfall of one million health professionals by 2020. In several European countries, foreign-born health care and social care workers are already in high demand as caregivers for older adults. In Southern European countries—especially in Italy—in-home care for older people by female migrant caregivers has become the main response to changing family roles, the increased labor force participation of women, and the inadequacy of formal care. In Western and Northern Europe—in Germany, Ireland, and Norway—an increasing reliance on foreign-born caregivers is emerging in the formal social care sector because of difficulties in recruiting native-born workers.

In theory, the remedy to labor shortages in the elder care sector, especially in long-term care, could be accomplished by increased wages and improved working conditions to make the jobs more attractive to the native-born workforce. However, employers in labor-intensive industries, such as long-term elder care, are reluctant to increase wages or non-wage labor costs—e.g., providing housing, meals, and increasing leave time—for fear of competitiveness and being priced out of the market. In this context, low-wage and flexible migrant labor seems like a better solution.

Many argue that migrant labor is needed in other industries as well, including agriculture, construction, hospitality, and high-tech industries.

Chapter 2

Scope of International Migration

The World Migration Report estimates that there were some 272 million international migrants in the world in 2019. This might sound like a large number, but in reality, it is a very small minority--3.5 percent to be exact--of the global population. It means that living in one's country of birth overwhelmingly remains the norm.

Nevertheless, the increase in the number of international migrants—both numerically and proportionally—has been evident over time. In 1990, there were 153 million international migrants compared to 84 million two decades earlier. While some think that the number of international migrants is increasing faster than previously predicted, the increase seems rather minimal. International migrants constituted 2.8 percent of the world's population in 2000; in 2019 they reached 3.5 percent (an increase of less than one percent in 20 years).

In 2019, Europe and Asia each hosted around 82 million and 84 million international migrants, respectively. These two regions comprised 61 percent of the total global international migrant stock combined. North America, with almost 59 million international migrants in 2019 or 22 percent of the global migrant stock, followed. Ten percent of all migrants were in Africa, four and three percent, respectively, of all international migrants resided in Latin America and the Caribbean, and Oceania.

When compared with the size of the population in each region, shares of international migrants in 2019 were highest in Oceania, North America, and Europe, where international migrants represented, respectively, 21 percent, 16 percent, and 11 percent of the total population. In Asia and Africa, the share of international migrants is relatively small: 1.8 and 2 percent, respectively. In Latin America and the Caribbean international migrants also constituted only 1.8 percent of the total population.

However, Asia, at 69 percent, experienced the most remarkable growth of international migrants between 2000 to 2019; this growth accounted for some 34 million people. Europe underwent the second largest growth during this period, with an increase of 25 million international migrants. The number of migrants increased by 18 million people in North America and 11 million in Africa.

'Stocks' and 'flows'

'Stocks' and 'flows' are basic demographic concepts used to analyze and understand migration processes in a country or region. Migration stocks are the numbers of migrants living in a country or region at any given point in time. Migration flows data capture the number of migrants entering and leaving (inflow and outflow) a country over the course of a specific period, such as one year. Data on migration flows are essential for understanding global migration patterns and how different factors and policies in countries of origin and destination may be related to flows. However, in contrast to migration stocks data, estimates on migration inflows and outflows by country of origin and destination are not available at the global level. Currently, only 45 countries report migration flow data to the United Nations.

Migration Data Portal

It is worthwhile to look at the gender composition of international migrants. For a long time, the prevailing assumption was that migrants are predominantly male. Feminization of international migration was not considered seriously until 1984 when Mirjana Morokvasic edited a special issue of the *International Migration Review* and demonstrated that 'birds of passage' were also female. The point she made was not so much that women migrants had to be 'rediscovered' but that the existing literature on migrating women had very little impact on policy-makers.

The feminization of migration is a multidimensional phenomenon. First, women are on the move as never before in history. In 2019, women comprised slightly less than half of all international migrants. The share of women in the total number of international migrants decreased from 49.3 percent in 2000 to 47.9 percent in 2019. The proportion of migrant women varied across regions. In 2019, the percentage of females among all international migrants was highest in North America (51.8 percent) and Europe (51.4 percent). Oceania, Latin America and the Caribbean, Central and Southern Asia, and Eastern and South-Eastern Asia hosted an almost equal proportion of female and male migrants. The proportion of female migrants was lowest in sub-Saharan Africa (47.5 percent) and Northern Africa and Western Asia (35.5 percent).

Second, there is a growing demand for migrant women's labor in destination countries, especially in the care, domestic, and manufacturing sectors. Millions of women from the Global South are migrating to do 'women's work' as the increased number of women in the Global North enter the labor market. Women working outside the home need help with raising children and attending to household needs. They hire migrant women to fulfill these jobs. Third, women are no longer migrating solely as part of a family; they have become independent migrants and/or primary economic providers. Currently, many more women move in search of jobs and better livelihoods than to join male family members. In 2016, women sent home $300.6 billion dollars; this amount represents half of the world remittances. This means that women move as much money as men, but at a greater percentage of their income, since they usually earn lower wages.

Migrants are usually quite young. The median age of international migrants worldwide was 39 years in 2019. International migrants living in sub-Saharan Africa were the youngest, with a median age of 30.9 years in 2019, followed by Latin America and the Caribbean (33.8 years), Northern Africa and Western Asia (34.0 years), and Eastern and South-Eastern Asia (35.7 years). In contrast, migrants were older in Central and Southern Asia (40.8 years), Europe (42.7 years), Oceania (42.9 years), and North America (43.5 years).

One out of every seven international migrants were below the age of 20. In 2019, the number of international migrants below age 20 reached 38 million, or 13.9 percent of the global migrant stock. Sub-Saharan Africa hosted the highest proportion of young people among all international migrants

(27.3 percent), followed by Latin America and the Caribbean, and Northern Africa and Western Asia (21.6 percent each). The share of those under age 20 among all migrants was smaller in Eastern and South-Eastern Asia (13.3 percent), Central and Southern Asia (13.2 percent), Oceania (11 percent), and Europe, and North America (8.8 percent each).

Three out of every four international migrants were of working age. This is not surprising, as many migrants leave their countries of origin in search of better livelihoods. In 2019, 202 million international migrants, equivalent to 74.2 percent of the global migrant stock, were between the ages of 20 and 64. More than three quarters of international migrants were of working age in Eastern and South-Eastern Asia (77.4 percent), Europe (76.8 percent), and Northern America (75.1 percent). In 2019, approximately 32 million international migrants, or 11.8 percent of the global migrant stock, were aged 65 years or over.

According to the United Nations, in 2017, around 11 percent of all international migrants were refugees and asylum-seekers. The number of refugees and asylum-seekers worldwide was nearly 29 million. Two thirds of all refugees and asylum-seekers lived in Northern Africa and Western Asia (13.1 million) and sub-Saharan Africa (5.9 million). Central and Southern Asia as well as Europe each hosted 3.6 million refugees and asylum-seekers. The remaining four regions hosted a combined total of 2.5 million refugees and asylum-seekers.

The prevailing assumption among many people is that international migration involves only movement from the Global South to the Global North. This is a very Western-centric viewpoint, often tied to the recent populist discourses about poor migrants 'invading' countries of the Global North. Nothing could be further from the truth, as evidenced by the numbers cited above.

The evidence is also on the ground. One only needs to go to Nepal and see how many Nepalese migrate not just to neighboring India, but also to the Gulf States. When I was conducting research in Nepal, there were whole villages that did not have any young residents as all the young people migrated in search of better economic prospects in the Middle East. The vast majority of passengers on flights from Kathmandu to Doha or Dubai were Nepali migrants.

Thailand, another country where I had done some research, has a long history of immigration. Thailand became a net immigration country in the early 1990s. Between 2000 and 2010, the foreign-born population increased by a factor of ten from 263,000 to 2.5 million people. Currently, there are almost 3 million registered migrant workers in Thailand, but the number of foreign-born people residing in the country is estimated at close to 5 million. Most of them come from neighboring Cambodia, Laos, Myanmar, and Vietnam. Thailand benefits significantly from their presence. Migrant workers help fill labor shortages, contribute to economic growth and are becoming ever more important as Thai society ages. Constituting over 10 percent of the total labor force, their work is thought to contribute between 4.3 to 6.6 percent of Thailand's Gross Domestic Product.

Migration scholars term these movements South-South migration. With the world's 82 million South-South migrants forming about 36 percent of the total stock of migrants, South-South migration is an increasingly significant factor in the economic and social development of many developing countries.

Another important fact to bear in mind is that the great majority of migrants do not migrate across international borders. Many more people migrate within countries. The International Organization for Migration (IOM) estimated that there were 740 million internal migrants in 2009. I have already mentioned internal migration in China. In the next section the reader will also learn about internal displacement within many armed conflict-ridden countries. Internally displaced persons outnumber refugees the same way internal migrants outnumber international migrants.

Chapter 3

Types of Migrants

Migration scholars and policy-makers use a variety of labels to categorize different strands of migration and migrants: labor migration, circular migration, voluntary migration, forced migration, migrant, immigrant, emigrant, refugee, asylum seeker, trafficked person, and more. Many of these labels have a long history of use. Some have roots in national laws, international conventions, bilateral agreements, and regional protocols defining migration patterns, categorizing migrants, and managing movement of people. Others have been coined by migration scholars.

However, there is no formal legal definition of international migration. Simply stated, migration is the movement of people from one place to live and work in another place. The International

Organization for Migration (IOM) defines a migrant as any person who has changed their country of usual residence, regardless of the reason for migration, the person's legal status, whether the movement is voluntary or involuntary, and what the length of the stay is. Generally, a distinction is made between short-term or temporary migration, covering movements with a duration between three and 12 months, and long-term or permanent migration, referring to a change of country of residence for a duration of one year or longer. Customarily, we call people leaving their homeland emigrants. People arriving in destination countries are called immigrants.

The broad label 'migrants' incorporates different types of people on the move. Let's look at some of them.

Displaced persons

Historically, 'displaced persons' or DPs were European refugees uprooted by World War II, the Holocaust, and the Soviet occupation of Central and Eastern Europe. WWII created some 60 million displaced persons worldwide, including approximately 30 million in Europe alone. There were 10 million displaced Germans. The term 'displaced persons' has subsequently been applied to many refugees uprooted by persecution, armed conflict, and natural disasters in different parts of the world. Displaced persons are involuntary migrants, forced to move from their homes and countries by extraordinary circumstances in search of safe haven. The U.N.'s refugee agency (UNHCR) reports that the number of displaced people has currently surpassed the post-World War II numbers, when the world was struggling to come to terms with the most devastating event in history. Filippo Grandi, the UN High Commissioner for Refugees, told reporters in Geneva that the global population of people displaced by conflict reached 70.8 million at the end of 2018, up from a little over 43 million a decade ago.

Refugees

Refugees are one category of displaced persons. The 1951 Convention relating to the Status of Refugees and its 1967 Optional Protocol constitute the main legal documents governing movement of refugees across international borders. The 1951 Convention established the definition of a refugee as well as the principle of *non-refoulement* and the rights afforded to those granted refugee status.

Refugee

Refugee is a person who is outside his/her country of nationality or habitual residence; has a well-founded fear of persecution because of his/her race, religion, nationality, membership in a particular social group or political opinion; and is unable or unwilling to avail himself/herself of the protection of that country, or to return there, for fear of persecution.

The 1951 Convention relating to the Status of Refugees

Non-refoulement

Non-refoulement is a fundamental principle of international law that forbids a country receiving asylum seekers from returning them to a country in which they would be in likely danger of persecution.

As of January 2020, there were 146 parties to the Convention and 147 to the Protocol. However, there are several countries, which are hosting large numbers of refugees, that have not signed the Refugee Convention, including Jordan and Turkey. Some countries signed the Convention but excluded refugees from being able to access certain services. Egypt, for example, limited refugees' access to employment and publicly-funded services. In view of these limitations, UNHCR and its partners subsidize health care, support education, and provide financial assistance to the most destitute refugees as well as those with special needs.

Although the 1951 Convention definition remains the dominant definition, regional human rights treaties have since modified the definition of a refugee in response to displacement crises not covered by the original convention. Countries in the Americas and Africa experiencing large-scale displacement as the result of armed conflicts decided that the 1951 Convention definition did not go far enough in addressing the protection needs of these populations. As a result, both the 1969 Organization of African Unity (OAU) Convention and the 1984 Cartagena Declaration expanded the definition of a refugee to include individuals who, owing to external aggression, occupation, foreign domination or events seriously disturbing public order in either part or the whole of their country of origin or nationality, are compelled to leave their place of habitual residence in order to seek refuge in another place outside their country of origin or nationality.

Half a century later, when large numbers of displaced persons are again seeking refuge, states have resorted to measures to circumvent their obligations under the Convention. These measures range from bilateral agreements condemning refugees to their vessels at sea to the excision of certain territories from national jurisdiction, limiting asylum seekers' ability to launch asylum claims, and building walls and fences to restrict them physically from crossing international borders.

Internally Displaced Persons

Internally displaced persons (IDPs) are in many ways similar to refugees. They too are forced to leave their homes in order to avoid the effects of armed conflicts, human rights violations, or natural and man-made disasters. However, in contrast to refugees, IDPs have not crossed an international border and remain within the borders of their countries of origin. The *United Nations Guiding Principles on Internal Displacement* provide a definition of IDPs.

Internally displaced people (IDPs)

Internally displaced people (IDPs) are persons or groups of persons who have been forced or obliged to flee or to leave their homes or places of habitual residence, in particular as a result of or in order to avoid the effects of armed conflict, situations of generalized violence, violations of human rights or natural or human-made disasters, and who have not crossed an internationally recognized state border.

UN Guiding Principles on Internal Displacement

This, however, is a descriptive definition, which does not confer a special legal status because IDPs, being inside their countries, at least in theory, remain entitled to all the rights and guarantees as citizens and other habitual residents of their countries. As such, national authorities have the primary responsibility to prevent forced displacement and to protect IDPs.

While the *UN Guiding Principles on Internal Displacement* are not legally binding, their authority has been recognized globally, particularly as they draw from international humanitarian and human rights law. The African Union, for example, has codified the UN Guiding Principles on Internal Displacement with the 2006 Great Lakes Protocol on the Protection and Assistance to Internally Displaced Persons and the 2009 Convention for the Protection and Assistance of Internally Displaced Persons in Africa (also known as the Kampala Convention).

According to the Internal Displacement Monitoring Center, the number of internally displaced persons (IDPs) reached a record high of 50.8 million people in 2019, an increase of 9.5 million from the previous year.

Asylum seekers

Many people often use the term refugee and asylum seeker interchangeably. This is technically incorrect. While every refugee is initially an asylum seeker, not all asylum seekers who launch asylum claims are granted refugee status. In fact, in many countries, approval rates of asylum applications are very low.

Asylum seeker

An **asylum seeker** is an individual who is seeking international protection. In countries with individualized procedures, asylum seekers are individuals whose claim has not yet been finally decided on by the country in which they launched their asylum application. Not every asylum seeker will ultimately be recognized as a refugee, but every refugee is initially an asylum seeker.

Amnesty International

Labor migrants

Many terms are used to describe people who move from one country to another for work. IOM differentiates between economic migrants and labor migrants. Those who move for the purpose of employment are considered labor migrants. Economic migrants form a broader group that includes investors and business people. The International Labor Organization (ILO) uses the term 'migrant worker' to describe individuals who migrate from one country to another with a view to being employed other than on their own account.

This category includes any person admitted as a migrant for employment whether they are high-skilled and high-paid workers or low-waged workers (often called low-skill migrants). This group also includes seasonal migrant workers and other temporary migrant workers.

In 2017, the ILO estimated that migrant workers accounted for 164 million of the world's approximately 258 million international migrants. Migrant workers contribute to growth and development in their countries of destination, while countries of origin greatly benefit from their remittances and the skills acquired during their migration experience. However, emigration of some workers results in what migration scholars call 'brain drain.' Researchers and the media have increasingly focused on the impact of international migration of nurses and its effects on the healthcare systems in their countries of origin. The World Health Organization (WHO) predicted a global shortage of nine million nurses and midwives by 2030 and called for an ethical recruitment of foreign nurses.

Human trafficking

The origins of contemporary conceptualizations and debates about human trafficking date back to the end of the nineteenth century when feminists such as Josephine Butler brought involuntary prostitution into the international discourse under the term 'White Slave Trade.' Many international agreements against 'white slavery' were passed, including the 1910 Mann Act in the United States, the 1933 International Convention for the Suppression of the Traffic in Women, and the 1949 UN Convention for the Suppression of Traffic in Persons and the Exploitation of the Prostitution of Others.

The most recent agreement is the *UN Protocol to Prevent, Suppress, and Punish Trafficking in Persons, Especially Women and Children*, also known as the *Palermo Protocol*, adopted by the UN General Assembly in November 2000. The Protocol was the target of heavy lobbying efforts by religious and feminist organizations, on the one hand, and human rights advocates, on the other hand. These two groups of activists represented two opposing views of prostitution. The Human Rights Caucus saw prostitution as legitimate labor, while the Coalition Against Trafficking in Women (CATW), representing religious and feminist activists, saw all prostitution as a violation of women's human rights. The CATW argued that trafficking should include all forms of recruitment and transportation for prostitution, regardless of whether force or deception took place. Meanwhile, the Human Rights Caucus, which supported the view of consensual prostitution as work, argued that force or deception was a necessary ingredient in the definition of human trafficking. The Caucus also maintained that the term 'human trafficking' should include trafficking of women, men, and children for different types of labor, including forced sweatshop labor, agriculture, and prostitution.

The two camps also presented differing views on the notion of consent. The CATW argued that prostitution is never voluntary, because women's consent to sex work is meaningless since they do not realize the exploitation they will experience. The Human Rights Caucus, on the other hand, posited that no one consents to abduction or forced labor, but an adult woman is able to consent to engagement in an illicit activity. If no one is forcing her to engage in such activity, then trafficking does not exist.

With this debate, the definition of trafficking became a battleground between those who consider it possible for sex work to be a voluntary choice and those who consider prostitution to always be forced. In the end, the signatories of the Palermo Protocol rejected the definition championed by the feminist and religious groups represented by the Coalition Against Trafficking in Women (CATW) and defined human trafficking as.

Human trafficking

(...) the recruitment, transportation, transfer, harboring or receipt of persons, by means of the threat or use of force or other forms of coercion, of abduction, of fraud, of deception, of abuse of power or of a position of vulnerability or of the giving or receiving of payments or benefits to achieve the consent of a person having control over another person, for the purpose of exploitation.

UN Palermo Protocol, 2000

Human smuggling

According to the *Smuggling of Migrants Protocol*, smuggling involves the facilitation of a person's illegal entry into a State, for a financial or other material benefit. It is often said that human smuggling is a crime against a state, while human trafficking is a crime against a person. However, smugglers can also violate the human rights of those they smuggle and abuse them physically and mentally.

Faced with increasing obstacles to access safety, refugees, asylum-seekers, and other persons in need of international protection are often compelled to use smugglers as their only means to flee persecution, conflict, and violence. Today, smugglers are often conflated with traffickers, especially in political discourses aimed at curtailing migration. It is easier,

I suppose, to convince the general public about the evils of human trafficking than admit that asylum seekers have few legal avenues to pursue and have to resort to clandestine migration.

What's in the name?

As already indicated, many of the categories used to describe different types of migration and different people on the move are defined in international, regional, and national legislation or protocols. Lawyers often argue the finer points of differences between trafficked victims or smuggled persons and between forced and voluntary migrant to obtain immigration relief for their clients, for whom a legal acknowledgment of a particular designation might mean safety from persecution or deportation to the dangerous situation they fled in the first place. This is no small matter in the court of immigration law or in a person's life.

Increasingly, however, these labels defy the complexity of contemporary mobility of people across international borders. The complexity of mobility blurs these seemingly elegant labels. Many scholars use the blurring of boundaries to problematize labels favored by policy-makers. The use of the categories 'refugee' and 'migrant' has featured prominently in the public debates during the most recent 'refugee crisis' in Europe, wrote Heaven Crawley and

Dimitris Skleparis. The authors blame what they call 'categorical fetishism' for failing to capture the complex relationship between political, social, and economic drivers of migration or their shifting significance for individuals over time and space.

What resonates the most with me in their argument is the usage of particular labels to justify policies of exclusion and containment. Those of us who have been in the refugee studies field for a long time remember the 1990s public debates and policies in the United Kingdom that made a distinction between 'deserving' refugees and the 'undeserving' asylum seekers, claiming that the majority of asylum seekers are 'bogus' and therefore undeserving of entry to Britain and of social support. Invoking Benedict Anderson, Chiara Marchetti reminds us that the polarity between deservingness and un-deservingness has another component, namely the imagined and socially constructed 'communities of value' populated by good, law-abiding citizens and hardworking members of stable and respectable families.' Unlike the Others, these ideal citizens share values and patterns of behaviors, form 'the legitimate us,' and have certain rights. In this conceptualization, terms like 'immigrant,' 'refugee,' and 'asylum seeker' are not simple descriptions of legal status but are value laden and negative terms.

In my own research on children and adolescents trafficked into the United States, I have underscored the fact that lived experiences of trafficked people—

and other types of migrants—unfold on a spectrum. Most of the young people I studied started as smuggled unaccompanied minors before their situation worsened and was deemed by the government or law enforcement to merit a label of trafficking. This did not necessarily mean that the young people identified as victims of trafficking or that they considered those who smuggled them across international borders as traffickers. Often the 'traffickers' were their parents or close acquaintances and the 'trafficking experience' was described as working.

Migrants toiling in the strawberry fields, men laboring in construction, and migrant women working as domestics are habitually called low-skill migrant workers. When I teach a class on labor migration, I ask my students if they can hang a drywall or deep clean a house. They stare at me and admit that they would not be able to perform these 'low-skill' tasks. They cannot lay bricks or mend a torn garment because these tasks demand quite sophisticated knowledge and a certain set of skills. These are not low-skill jobs, these are low-paid jobs, because we—people with college degrees—don't value these skills, or worse, want to exploit brown and black bodies and pay them meager wages for jobs that we cannot do but want done.

Finally, I think it is important to ask migrants what word they prefer to describe their migration experiences. I come from Poland, but when I sought refuge in the United States in the early 1980s, I was immediately called 'New American.' I did not like this label at first, as my Polish identity was still very strong, but I learnt to appreciate it as my migration journey unfolded. I took my oath to become a U.S. citizen in 1998 in front of an African American judge alongside 97 other New Americans representing several dozen countries of origin. My daughter, Marta, is a Washington D.C.-native, holds dual citizenship, and knows no Polish, but speaks fluent Spanish with an Argentine accent. Despite having a foreign-born mother, she has never been perceived as an immigrant by mainstream society. She is a second-generation U.S. citizen. The Latino children she teaches in Queens call her *gringa* (foreigner), but are proud that their teacher—although not a Latina—speaks Spanish. Despite the fact that, like Marta, many of them were born in the United States, they are often thought of as immigrants. Birthright citizenship accords both Marta and her students U.S. citizenship at birth regardless of the immigration status of their parents, but white privilege protects Marta from being labelled an immigrant while her students of color continue to be othered no matter their place of birth.

Chapter 4

Nations of Immigrants: the United States, Canada, and Australia

The United States, Canada, and Australia have long been considered nations of immigrants. While there are some similarities between these countries, there are also vast differences regarding admission of immigrants and refugees, provision of rights, access to public services, and integration policies.

United States

The United States has more immigrants than any other country in the world. Today, some 45 million people living in the U.S. were born in another country. That accounts for about one-fifth of the world's migrants. Immigrants to the United States include both documented and undocumented migrants, refugees and labor migrants, adults and children, children who migrate as part of a family unit, and adolescents who migrate by themselves.

Documented immigrants

More than one million immigrants arrive in the U.S. each year. Since 1965, when U.S. immigration laws replaced a national quota system, the number of immigrants living in the U.S. has more than quadrupled. Immigrants today account for 13.7 percent of the U.S. population, nearly triple the share (4.8 percent) in 1970. However, today's immigrant share remains below the record 14.8 percent share in 1890, when 9.2 million immigrants lived in the country.

The vast majority of immigrants (77 percent) are in the country legally, while almost a quarter are unauthorized, according to the Pew Research Center estimates. In 2017, 45 percent of all immigrants were naturalized U.S. citizens. Some 27 percent of immigrants were permanent residents and five percent were temporary residents.

The population of immigrants is also very diverse, with just about every country in the world represented among U.S. immigrants. In 2018, the top country of origin for new immigrants coming into the U.S. was China, with 149,000 people, followed by India (129,000), Mexico (120,000) and the Philippines (46,000). By race and ethnicity, more Asian immigrants than Hispanic immigrants have arrived in the U.S. in most years since 2009. Asians are projected to become the largest immigrant group in the U.S. by 2055, surpassing Hispanics. Pew Research Center estimates indicate that in 2065, those who identify as Asian will make up some 38 percent of all immigrants; as Hispanic, 31 percent; White, 20 percent; and Black, 9 percent.

Nearly half of the nation's immigrants live in just three states: California (24 percent), Texas (11 percent), and Florida (10 percent). California had the largest immigrant population of any state in 2018, at 10.6 million. Texas, Florida, and New York had more than four million immigrants each. Following historical patterns, many immigrants continue to settle in traditional gateway cities such as New York, Chicago, Boston, Los Angeles, Dallas, and Miami. However, starting in the 1980s researchers noticed a growing number of immigrants moving to communities with little recent history of immigration. New settlement areas outside the core immigration states grew by 45 percent in the 1980s and an astonishing 94 percent in the 1990s.

The roots of today's new settlements are complex. In some cases, businesses actively recruited immigrants into new communities. During the 1980s, meat processing plants began to relocate from north central states to south central states to recruit non-union, low-wage workers. Establishing themselves in rural communities with limited labor force, processing companies had recruited immigrant workers from California and Texas as well as directly from Mexico and Central America. Communities such as Rogers, Arkansas; Georgetown, Delaware; and Faribault, Minnesota now have sizable immigrant communities.

Undocumented migrants

In addition to immigrants (naturalized citizens, permanent and temporary residents) living lawfully in the country, approximately 23 percent of all immigrants are unauthorized immigrants. From 1990 to 2007, the unauthorized immigrant population more than tripled in size – from 3.5 million to a record high of 12.2 million in 2007. By 2017, that number had declined by 1.7 million, or 14 percent. There were 10.5 million unauthorized immigrants in the U.S. in 2017, accounting for 3.2 percent of the nation's population.

The decline in the unauthorized immigrant population is due largely to a fall in the number of immigrants from Mexico – the single largest group of unauthorized immigrants in the United States. Between 2007 and 2017, this group decreased by 2 million. Meanwhile, there was a rise in the number of migrants from Central America and Asia.

While several presidents and immigrant advocates pushed for immigration reforms to regularize undocumented immigrants, the United States has not seen any legislative action focused on this population since the 1986 Immigration Reform and Control Act (IRCA), which provided legal status to 2.7 million immigrants.

Two surveys conducted in 1989 and 1992 suggested that immigrants made significant wage gains in the years after legalization, many of them by obtaining better jobs. Government records also revealed over time how many of them became naturalized citizens. In 1996, the year the entire IRCA cohort was eligible, a quarter of a million were naturalized. By 2001, one-third of the entire group had become U.S. citizens.

More recently, President Barack Obama made several attempts to have the U.S. Congress consider comprehensive immigration reform, including a path to citizenship for millions of undocumented migrants residing in the United States. His efforts were met with fierce political opposition. In the end, unable to pass new legislation, in 2012 President Obama issued an executive order temporarily protecting young undocumented migrants. Known by its acronym, DACA or Deferred Action for Childhood Arrivals, this directive provided temporary work permits and deportation relief to some 664,000 young undocumented immigrants who had lived in the United States since childhood.

Two years later, in 2014, President Obama issued another executive order, called DAPA or Deferred Action for Parents of Americans and Lawful Permanent Residents. This provision was for undocumented immigrants who had lived in the United States since 2010 and had children who were either American citizens or lawful permanent residents. It was prevented from going into effect. Several states filed lawsuits against the federal government, arguing that DAPA violates the Constitution and federal statutes. A temporary injunction was issued in February 2015, blocking the program from going into effect. The Fifth Circuit Court of Appeals affirmed, and a U.S. Supreme Court 4–4 split decision in June 2016 effectively left the block in place.

On his first day in office, President Biden announced the highlights of a far-reaching plan to reform the U.S. immigration system. The anticipated bill is expected to feature a path to permanent residence and citizenship for qualifying undocumented foreign nationals and those holding Deferred Action for Childhood Arrivals (DACA), Temporary Protected Status (TPS), and H-2A status; mechanisms to clear extensive green card backlogs in the employment-based and family-based programs; a streamlined process for graduates of U.S. universities with advanced STEM degrees to obtain permanent residence; and an increase in Diversity Lottery Visas, among other provisions.

Refugees

The modern history of refuge in the United States goes back to the Displaced Persons Act of 1948, which many consider the beginning of the U.S. refugee resettlement program. This does not mean that those fleeing persecution did not seek refuge in the country before 1948. Many did; some successfully, others not. Probably the most infamous rejection of refugees trying to enter the United States is represented by the ill-fated voyage of the St. Louis, carrying onboard 900 mostly German Jews fleeing the Nazi regime in 1939. In the same year, an attempt to allow 20,000 German Jewish refugee children was also rebuffed.

In contrast to widespread indifference towards refugees before World War II, the situation changed after the war. In 1945, President Harry Truman went behind the backs of an anti-immigrant Congress and xenophobic country and issued The Truman Directive. Twenty-three thousand unwanted Jewish refugees entered America in 1946 under his executive order. Three years later, following constant pressure from the White House, Congress finally passed the Displaced Persons Act of 1948. As welcome as this legislation was, it fell short of its more inclusive aims.

The Displaced Persons Act authorized admissions of refugees from Europe and permitted asylum seekers already in the United States to regularize their status. It provided for admission of 200,000 displaced persons and attempted to favor Catholic and Protestant refugees over Jewish ones by enacting preferences for agricultural workers. Although Asians received no refugee visas, the Act enabled several thousand Chinese already residing in the United States to gain legal permanent status by claiming asylum. Many were highly educated and well connected, with skills and knowledge considered strategic for the United States, and worth keeping away from the communist side. The Displaced Persons Act expired at the end of 1952.

On August 7, 1953, President Dwight D. Eisenhower signed into law the Refugee Relief Act to supplant the Displaced Persons Act. The new legislation resulted in the admission of 214,000 immigrants to the United States, including 60,000 Italians, 17,000 Greeks, 17,000 Dutch, and 45,000 men, women, and children from countries under communist control. Upon signing the new law, Eisenhower said: "In enacting this legislation, we are giving a new chance in life to 214,000 fellow humans."

Not everybody was as enthusiastic as President Eisenhower about the new law. Senator Pat McCarran (D-Nevada) argued that amendments that required applicants to undergo an in-depth security screening should be added. In seeking to block increased immigration, McCarran argued that many immigrants already in the United States are not well-integrated, emphasizing lack of capacity to resettle any additional newcomers.

A few years later, the same desire to protect refugees escaping a communist regime governed the resettlement of Hungarians fleeing the Soviet repression of the 1956 Hungarian revolution. Some 200,000 Hungarians fled the country as Soviet tanks rolled into Budapest to crush, once and for all, a national uprising. Most fled to nearby Austria, but the United States brought in 38,000 Hungarians within the span of three months. The Hungarian resettlement process represented a novel approach to immigration policy. Instead of the legislative branch, it was the White House that took charge of the effort. Moreover, local integration was facilitated by the National Academy of Sciences as most of the refugees were scientists and students.

On November 8, 1956, the U.S. government announced that 5,000 'escapee visas' would be made available for the Hungarian refugees per the Refugee Relief Act of 1953, which was about the expire at the end of December. Over 6,000 Hungarians were admitted with escapee visas. The rest entered under the parole provision of the Immigration and Nationality Act, also known as the McCarran-Walter Act. Originally, the parolees were allowed to live and work in the United States, but were not given a formal immigrant status until July 1958, through legislative action, when it became clear that they would not return to Hungary any time soon.

Twenty-seven years after the Displaced Persons Act of 1948, in response to the large numbers of refugees created by the Vietnam War, the Indochina Migration and Refugee Assistance Act of 1975 created a domestic resettlement program for Vietnamese and Cambodian refugees. Laotians were made eligible for the program a year later, in 1976. However, it was not until 1980 that a fully-fledged refugee resettlement program was created. The Refugee Act of 1980 established a domestic resettlement program for all refugees. It defined 'refugee' in accordance with the 1967 United Nations Protocol on Refugees as a person with well-founded fear of persecution for reasons of race, religion, nationality, membership in a particular social group or political opinion, and removed refugees from the immigration preference system.

The Refugee Act of 1980 established a formal U.S. refugee resettlement system with a network of agencies that have formed a public-private partnership with the U.S. government, including the U.S. State Department for the admission of refugees and initial reception and placement services and with the U.S. Office of Refugee Resettlement (ORR) for continued services. Prior to 2017, the network included 325 local agencies serving refugees in every state of the Union except Wyoming.

The Refugee Act also established that the President, in consultation with Congress, is responsible for setting the number of refugees to be admitted to the country each fiscal year. The U.S. has historically led the world in refugee resettlement. Between 1980 and 2018, the United States has resettled three million of the more than four million refugees resettled worldwide, admitting on average 80,000 refugees annually, with as many as 200,000 a year in the early 1980s.

For 40 years the U.S. refugee resettlement program enjoyed bi-partisan support from Congress and six successive U.S. presidents. Congress continues to provide bi-partisan support to the refugee resettlement program as evidenced by the recent revival of the bi-partisan Refugee Caucus in the U.S. House of Representatives. In 2018, members of the Refugee Caucus urged the president to maintain the U.S. Refugee Admissions Program and for the administration to set a level for accepting refugees that "will continue to align with global need and signal to the international community that the U.S. will continue to be a global leader in refugee protection." A year later, it seems that this call to action has fallen on deaf ears.

Before I discuss the Trump administration's attempts to de facto shut down the refugee resettlement program, it is prudent to mention other factors that have contributed to the slow erosion of the program aimed at protecting and ensuring security of refugees and asylum seekers. I have to mention, however briefly, the chilling effects of the terrorist attacks on the United States on September 11, 2001, on refugee admissions. It is also worth bringing up 'expedited removal,' a provision stemming from the Illegal Immigration Reform and Immigrant Responsibility Act (IRIRA) of 1996, and the continued erosion of the Temporary Protected Status (TPS).

The chilling effect of 9/11 on refugee admissions
Only once in the history of U.S. refugee resettlement was the program shut down. Two weeks after the terrorist attacks on September 11, 2001, a plane full of Afghan refugees arrived at John F. Kennedy Airport (JFK). Many such planes landed at JFK before 9/11. However, this time airport officials alerted Mayor Giuliani's office and stated that hundreds of Afghans had just landed in New York City. Alarmed, the Mayor called Vice President Dick Cheney and within days the U.S. refugee resettlement program, the first refugee protection casualty of the terrorist attacks, was shut down. The Vice President and other American officials perceived resettlement as being particularly vulnerable to security problems. They contended that the refugee and asylum programs could be exploited by terrorist networks. The arrest in May 2011 of two Iraqi refugees in Kentucky for conspiring to provide weapons to Al Qaeda indicate that some vulnerabilities persist. Nonetheless, the chance of being killed on U.S. soil in a terrorist attack committed by a refugee was 1 in 3.86 billion a year.

The total shut down of the program was brief --three months-- while security measures were examined. But three years later the program was still operating at only about two-thirds of its previous capacity. Despite the sharp decline in refugee resettlement in the immediate period following 9/11, the U.S. managed to resettle more refugees (33,000) than any other single country during that time.

Following the U.S. were Canada (27,000), Australia (15,000), and the United Kingdom (6,000). Sweden, Germany, Norway, and France each resettled about 3,000 refugees. The refugee admissions had rebounded to nearly 75,000 per year by fiscal years 2009 and 2010, before falling below 75,000 in fiscal year 2011. The Obama administration's goal was to admit 110,000 refugees in fiscal year 2017, which would have been the highest number since 1994. In the last year of the Obama administration, the U.S. resettled close to 85,000 refugees, a few thousand short of the original goal.

The faltering U.S. protection for refugees and asylum seekers

For many years, the U.S. has also granted political asylum to more than 20,000 persons each year, extended temporary protected status (TPS) to tens of thousands of foreign nationals fearing return to their home countries because of armed conflict, egregious abuses of human rights, or natural disasters, and offered protection to survivors of human trafficking. However, despite its generosity, the U.S. refugee protection system has been eroding in recent years.

Post 9/11 security measures, combined with U.S. interdiction policies, have prevented many asylum-seekers from reaching safe haven in the U.S. The 'expedited removal' process, a procedure, created in 1996 by the Illegal Immigration Reform and Immigration Responsibility Act (IIRAIRA), that allows U.S. Customs and Border Protection (CBP) officials to rapidly deport non-citizens who are undocumented or who have committed misrepresentation or fraud, has expanded considerably over the years. In order to avoid summary removal, migrants must express a fear of persecution or request political asylum to an immigration officer. If they ask for political asylum, they are supposed to be interviewed by an asylum officer from the U.S. Citizenship and Immigration Service (USCIS). The goal of this interview is to determine whether they indeed have a 'credible fear' of persecution. During the 'credible fear' process, they must be detained. However, the U.S. Commission on International Religious Freedom (USCIRF) found that in one of every six cases in which migrants expressed a fear of return they did not receive 'credible fear' interviews and were removed in contravention of the law.

The most recent expansion of the expedited removal happened on July 23, 2019, when the Department of Homeland Security (DHS) announced that most undocumented persons who cannot prove they have resided in the United States for more than two years will be subject to expedited removal. Immigrant rights advocates have previously expressed concerns about the lack of due process involved in expedited removal, both at designated ports of entry and for people in the border zone. The American Civil Liberties Union (ACLU) has argued that expedited removal can lead to deportation of many people who would qualify for asylum. The ACLU has also noted that the 100-mile 'border zone' within which expedited removal can be carried out houses roughly two-thirds of the United States population, and has expressed concern about the implications of these broad enforcement powers for civil rights and constitutional protections. The Immigration Policy Council noted that expedited removal proceedings and other rapid deportation decisions fail to take into account many critical factors, including whether the individual is eligible to apply for lawful status in the United States, whether he or she has long-standing ties here, or whether he or she has U.S.-citizen family members.

In 2015, the U.S. House of Representatives voted 289–137 to pass the American Security Against Foreign Enemies Act of 2015, also known as the SAFE Act. The SAFE Act specifically singled out refugees coming from Syria or Iraq. The Act was created in response to the November 2015 Paris attacks, out of concern that ISIL terrorists would enter the United States posing as refugees fleeing Syria. The attacks have turned possible admission of refugees fleeing war-torn Syria and Iraq into a high-stakes political issue.

The Act was met with many criticisms. Democrats opposing the Republican bill said the U.S. has no business abandoning its age-old values, including being a safe haven for people fleeing countries racked by violence. The then FBI Director, James Comey, posited that the SAFE Act micromanaged the process in a way that is counter-productive to national security. The American Civil Liberties Union (ACLU) called the measure 'un-American' and said it would bring U.S. resettlement of refugees to a grinding halt. The U.S. Holocaust Memorial Museum weighed in on the discussions and drew a comparison between Syrian refugees unable to enter the United States and Jews who were unable to flee Nazism.

Conflating refugees with terrorists

Imagining that traffickers infiltrate refugee populations and place terrorists among them, Donald Trump lowered the refugee admission cap from 110,000 to 45,000. He later reduced the cap to 30,000 people, and most recently set it at 18,000 individuals — the lowest in the history of the refugee resettlement program.

On January 27, 2017, Donald Trump signed Executive Order 13769 entitled Protecting the Nation from Foreign Terrorist Entry into the United States. The order denied for 120 days the entry of refugees and banned for 90 days the entry into the United States of individuals from seven predominantly Muslim countries: Iran, Iraq, Libya, Somalia, Sudan, Syria, and Yemen. Many criticized the executive order. Some 1,000 U.S. diplomats signed a dissent cable opposing the order, setting a record. Public opinion was divided, with initial national polls yielding inconsistent results, from 57 percent of the polled respondents favoring the ban (Rasmussen poll) to the same percentage opposing it (Gallup poll), and others being split (Reuters). The inconsistencies stemmed from the questions asked in the polls. The Rasmussen poll asked whether people favored a temporary ban from seven countries until the government improves its screening for potential terrorists; the Reuters poll asked whether people agreed or disagreed with an order signed by Trump blocking refugees and banning people from seven Muslim-majority countries; and the Gallup poll asked whether people approved of Trump ordering a temporary ban for most people from seven predominantly Muslim countries.

Thousands of protesters gathered at airports across the country on the Sunday following the signing of the executive order. The ban, which took effect immediately upon its signing, caused sudden chaos at U.S. airports and resulted in the removal of some arriving non-immigrants and the revocation of more than 60,000 visas. Dulles airport serving the Washington D.C. area was a place of tense scenes among protesters, Democratic congressmen, and transit officials. Among those detained at airports were numerous U.S. permanent residents; in some cases, they were held for up to 30 hours despite the fact that the White House Chief of Staff indicated that green card holders were exempted from the executive order.

The order quickly became subject to multiple legal challenges. The Muslim American Society was one of the organizations challenging the order. Several federal courts temporarily restrained or enjoined parts of the executive order. In order to avoid these legal pitfalls, the order was revised several times over the next year and a half. Executive Order 13780, with the same title, was signed on March 6, 2017. The new order delayed the implementation date and exempted individuals who were previously authorized to travel to the United States. The day before the new order was to take effect, it became subject to a nationwide temporary restraining order. However, the Supreme Court later allowed for partial implementation with respect to foreigners without a *bona fide* relationship with a U.S.-based individual or entity, indicating that the administration was successful in avoiding legal challenges. The Supreme Court's decision has given some Transportation Security Administration and Customs & Border Control officers the liberty to discriminate against Muslims, detaining them or putting them through unwarranted secondary screening at ports of entry around the U.S.

The executive orders paved the way for further erosion of the refugee resettlement program. In addition to lowering the cap on the number of admitted refugees by 40 percent in just one year, the Trump administration also allowed local jurisdictions more leeway in rejecting refugees who are being resettled across the country. Some experts assert that such powers are less relevant at a time when very few refugees are being admitted. I wonder, however, how this new power given to states and localities might affect refugees already resettled in the United States. Will discrimination against refugees increase? Will violence follow?

In a recent opinion piece published in *The Washington Post*, former vice president Walter Mondale recalled a day some 40 years ago when he stood before the Geneva Meeting on Refugees and Displaced Persons in South-East Asia at a time when hundreds of thousands of women, men, and children fled the south of Vietnam. The conference Mondale was addressing, convened by the United Nations, was a wake-up call meant to draw the attention of the world to a horrific humanitarian crisis. Following the conference, the U.S. Refugee Act of 1980 was signed into law by President Jimmy Carter. The act received full bipartisan support in the Senate before President Carter signed it. The act tripled the number of refugees the United States would admit, and, most importantly, amended the definition of refugee to include someone with "well-founded fear of persecution." In his op-ed, Walter Mondale bemoaned the fact that Donald Trump "has twisted the perception of refugees and asylum seekers into an unrecognizable lie. But here are the facts: Asylum seekers and refugees leave their countries because they have no choice — for many, if they stay, they will be persecuted, subjected to traumatic events such as torture, or killed." Mondale reminded us that refugees and asylum seekers have the legal right to seek protection from persecution.

This includes the asylum seekers at the U.S. southern border with Mexico. However, the Trump administration considers all asylum seekers traveling through Mexico by land to the southern border ineligible for asylum if they have not first sought protection there before reaching the U.S. Hundreds of thousands of Central Americans and others have been affected by the restrictions that took effect in July 2019. This policy has enraged many refugee and migration advocates, but it has also angered asylum officers. The labor union which represents them has filed a fourth amicus brief since January 2017 in the 9th Circuit Court of Appeals in opposition to the administration's cruel and harmful asylum policies. In June 2020, the Trump administration proposed a new asylum law that would make it virtually impossible for many people, including women and children, fleeing gang and domestic violence to obtain asylum in the United States.

The question remains: Is refugee protection incompatible with national security? The one-word answer is: No. Interpreted broadly, national security refers to more than national defense, strong military, secure borders, absence of wars. It also refers to the protection of a people, territory, and way of life. Rather than being perceived as a threat, a robust refugee protection system can positively influence economic, military, and diplomatic state powers. In a globalized world, economic prosperity of one nation is not possible without contact with the rest of the world. Refugees contribute to the economic prosperity of resettlement countries where they pay taxes and origin countries through remittances.

Canada

The United States might be the quintessential nation of immigrants, but the proportion of the foreign-born in Canada is actually higher than in the United States. According to the 2016 Canadian Census, 21.9 percent of the Canadian population was foreign-born, while the proportion of the foreign-born in the U.S. has hovered around 13 percent. In absolute numbers, the foreign-born population of Canada included 7,540,830 people. Among immigrants living in Canada in 2016, 1,212,075 came between 2011 and 2016. These recent immigrants made up 16.1 percent of Canada's immigrant population. This represents a decrease since 2010, when 19 percent of the Canadian population of 34 million was foreign-born.

The immigrant population of Canada is very diverse. Newcomers to Canada hail from 200 different countries. In 2010, the foreign-born include 34 distinct ethnic groups of at least 100,000 members each. Over 58 percent of immigrants come from Asia, mainly from China, India, the Philippines, Pakistan, South Kora, and Sri Lanka.

Ethnic composition of immigrant communities is important, especially for Quebec. Traditionally, Quebec has been concerned that immigrants embrace the francophone institutions and cultural values in order to enhance the French-Canadian character of the province. There is some evidence that Quebec has done outreach to French-speaking Africans to attract them to settle in Quebec.

In the United States, immigration policy is solely in the purview of the federal government. The 1867 Canadian Constitution stipulated that the central government and the four original provinces shared responsibility for immigration matters, with the federal government having primacy in this area. The 1982 Canada Constitutional Act confirmed this dual responsibility in determining annual admission levels and provided further legal grounds for cooperation between Ottawa and the 10 provincial authorities.

Prior to the 1960s, considerations of race, ethnicity, religion, gender, sexual orientation, and national origin greatly affected the Canadian immigration selection processes. Canadian policy-makers defined Canada as a 'white man's country' and used immigration to promote this ideal. Before the 1960s, when the demand for cheap immigrant labor clashed with the vision of the ideal settler and a future citizen of Canada, gendered immigration policies focused on the recruitment of male laborers. Women from unwanted ethnic groups such as East and South Asian and Blacks were considered inadmissible. Gendered and highly racialized immigration policies focused instead on the recruitment of 'respectable' white French and British female migrants arriving in Canada with husbands or on 'bride ships.' World War II, the human rights movement, and the discreditation of 'scientific racism' prompted the country to move to an admission system based on education, skills, and other forms of human capital.

In the recent past, Canada admitted approximately 240,000 immigrants a year, divided into three major categories: family reunification (30 percent), refugees (20 percent), and economic immigrants (50 percent). According to the Immigration, Refugees and Citizenship Departmental Plan 2020-2021, Canada plans to increase permanent resident admissions to 341,000 in 2020 and 350,000 in 2021. The Department will also continue to explore and develop new ways to select permanent residents in response to specific regional and labor sector needs, such as the Atlantic Immigration Pilot, Rural and Northern Immigration Pilot, Municipal Nominee Program, Agri-Food Immigration Pilot, and Home Child Care Provider and Home Support Worker pilots. Most of the increase in immigration levels planned for 2020 and 2021 will be allocated to economic immigration, under the federal high-skilled category.

Merit-based system

Canada implemented a points system in 1967, the merit-based system, in order to move away from origin-based selection of immigrants. Under this system, economic immigration candidates are evaluated and ranked using a 100-point selection factor grid that considers factors such as age, education, work specialization, work experience in Canada and abroad as well as arranged employment in Canada.

Applicants to the federal skilled workers program are further ranked according to a 1,200-point Comprehensive Ranking System (CRS).

Would-be immigrants to Canada are also evaluated for adaptability, measured by elements such as past experiences in Canada, but also by the presence of relatives in the country and their spouses' language proficiency.

So even when measuring for 'merit,' the Canadian immigration system does include a recognition of the importance of family ties and social networks. What's more, not all individuals who enter Canada through the economic class are selected using the economic criteria. Between 2006 and 2015, only 41 to 49 percent of these individuals were selected directly based on their potential for contributing to the Canadian economy. The rest of the economic class is comprised of close family members of the main applicant.

The merit-based system has met with some criticism. Restricting immigration to young and skilled immigrants succeeds in selecting economically desirable immigrants and provides orderly management of population growth. However, the point system can neither fix short-term skilled labor shortages in a timely manner nor prevent poor labor market outcomes for immigrants, since domestic employers can undervalue schooling and work experience acquired abroad. Furthermore, the efficacy of a point system can be compromised if unscreened visa categories receive higher priority.

Using a point system for selecting immigrants

Pros	Cons
• A point system acts as an effective binding constraint on applicants.	• Comprehensive and regular data collection is needed for policy evaluation and fine-tuning.
• Individual applicants are selected according to the objectives set by the country of destination.	• Applicants are selected solely from observable characteristics, not from unobservables like innate ability or attitude.
• A point system elicits better quality immigration candidates.	• Successful applicants may still end up in jobs and at pay levels below their true potential.
• The initial phase of the immigration process is streamlined, requiring fewer resources to process valid applications.	• A point system is unsuitable for providing fast responses to skill shortages in the domestic labor market.
• The assessment process is transparent.	• The effectiveness of a point system can be compromised if higher priority is given to unscreened classes of applicants.

Massimiliano Tani
UNSW Canberra, Australia, and IZA, Germany

Private sponsorship of refugees

In 2019, Canada resettled 30,100 refugees, far exceeding the United States and Australia in the number of refugees admitted that year. Canada plans to resettle over 30,000 refugees in 2020. While the admission levels are commendable, about three in five refugees who have arrived in Canada over the past decade have been admitted under the private sponsorship program. Private sponsorship was formalized by the 1976 Immigration Act, drawing on the will of private individuals to identify and support refugees financially and emotionally for one year by taking responsibility for their resettlement and integration. The Canadian private sponsorship program is the oldest in the world and has offered protection to more than 350,000 refugees. Originally, the private sponsorship was intended to be complementary to the federal resettlement program but has begun to outpace it in recent years.

Criticism has greeted the shifting balance between the federal program and private sponsorship. The incidence of sponsorship breakdown has grown, with sponsors unable or unwilling to provide the promised support until the end of the sponsorship period. Indeed, the Quebec government suspended private sponsorship by organizations for a year after receiving serious allegations about the program. The question remains: is reliance on private sponsorship sustainable?

Multiculturalism underpins contemporary Canadian immigration and refugee policy and defines the Canadian society and identity. Federal multiculturalism policy will mark its 50th anniversary in 2021. It was adopted in 1971 by Pierre Trudeau's Liberal government. An unexpected by-product of the Royal Commission on Bilingualism and Biculturalism (1963–69), multiculturalism was intended as a policy solution to manage both rising francophone nationalism, particularly in Quebec, and increasing cultural diversity across the country. Canada was the first country in the world to adopt a policy of multiculturalism.

Given Canada's early racist tendencies, the establishment of multiculturalism was a remarkable shift in public thinking. While many prize multiculturalism, some argue that multiculturalism is a pernicious ideology that enforces the ghettoization of those different from the mainstream. The critics fear that the policy is divisive because it emphasizes what is different, rather than shared Canadian values. Canadian culture and symbols, it is felt, are being discarded in the effort to accommodate other cultures. On the other hand, defenders of Canada's approach to multiculturalism argue that it encourages integration by telling immigrants they do not have to choose between preserving their linguistic and cultural heritage and participating in Canadian society. Rather, they can do both.

Australia

Australia is also a major immigrant receiving country. In 2019, there were over 7.5 million migrants living in the country accounting for 29.7 percent of the total population. This is the highest proportion of the foreign-born among the three nations of immigrants. The history of immigration policy in Australia includes both harsh race and ethnicity-based selectivity among migrants and active promotion of migration policy through government policies.

Until the 1960s, Australia was preoccupied with maintaining its British identity in public and private spheres. Throughout the twentieth century, Britain's colonial legacy, Australia's relationship with Asia, and perceptions of whiteness and blackness influenced Australian migration policy. The 'White Australia' policy was central to the country's immigration policy. Literacy tests controlled the entry of non-white immigrants. Removal of 'non-white' immigrants already in Australia was also an important feature of the policy. It affected especially the Chinese and the Pacific Islanders. The Chinese had a long history of working in the marine industries and in mining in the northern parts of Australia. The Pacific Islanders were concentrated in northern Queensland where they worked mainly in the sugar cane industry. Many non-white immigrants were deported, but some tried to blend in and adhere to the Anglo-Australian norms. Very few were successful as deliberate discrimination of non-white settlers worked against them.

World War I disrupted immigration to Australia. Immigrants began arriving again after the war once shipping became available. In the post-WWI period, migration to rural areas was encouraged. When the 1924 Johnson-Reed Act imposed quotas on the number of immigrants allowed to enter the United States, large numbers of immigrants were diverted to Australia. Many of them were Italian and although Italians obviously identified as Europeans, Australians did not consider them fully white.

Fears about migration continued. Beyond the concerns related to whiteness, the social debates also centered on moral contagion, especially during the Depression of the 1930s. Fears were connected to both the right-wing governments in Germany and Italy as well as left-wing sympathies expressed by some immigrants. These fears continued after the outbreak of War World II. Both the Australian government and the general population were concerned about potential fifth columnists. Just like in the United States and Canada, many immigrants and citizens hailing from enemy countries were interned.

Following the end of WWII, the Australian government sought to expand immigration to Australia. Having seen Britain's inability to defend Australia and shocked by the Japanese war-time advance, the Australian government aimed to bring in a sufficient number of immigrants to defend the continent. The immigration minister, Arthur Caldwell, first looked towards traditional immigrant-sending countries, but in light of insufficient numbers of volunteers, the government also looked towards displaced persons in camps throughout Europe. Those who fled communist countries were encouraged to immigrate to Australia, while those with socialist backgrounds were denied entry.

Government sponsored migration programs offered many incentives, including cheap shipping fees, to would-be immigrants. Many of these schemes were later criticized, including programs focused on bringing in children. In 2010, both the Australian and the British government extended a formal apology to the postwar child immigrants.

Despite the focus on 'White Australia,' immigrants to Australia were becoming more and more heterogenous. In 1973, the shift away from the 'White Australia' policy and the assimilationist model was formalized. A new multicultural model was implemented. It aimed to improve social welfare through linguistically appropriate and culturally sensitive delivery of services. However, migrants from Asia and Arab countries were viewed as problematic and were criminalized in public debates.

Historically, Australia was viewed as a world leader in refugee resettlement, following the United States and Canada. In the 1930s, Australia accepted more than 7,000 refugees from Nazi Germany. Following the end of World War II almost 200,000 European refugees settled in Australia.

Australia is a signatory to the 1951 Convention Relating to the Status of Refugees and the 1967 Protocol, but has had a very poor track record of accepting refugees, especially those who arrived by boats. Starting in July 2013, Australia has forcibly transferred more than 3,000 asylum seekers who traveled there by boat to camps on Papua New Guinea and Nauru.

The country vowed that asylum seekers who arrived by boat would never be allowed to settle in Australia. Successive Australian governments have defended that policy, claiming that it has deterred both asylum seekers and traffickers who profit from their misery, saving lives at sea. This 'experiment' has not worked. Seven years later, in 2020, more than 370 people still choose to endure horrific hardship in Papua New Guinea and Nauru rather than return to conflict and persecution in their home countries. They languish in limbo, separated from families, futures uncertain.

The United States took more than 700 people in a resettlement arrangement with Australia, and over the years the Australian government reluctantly transferred more than 1,200 asylum seekers and refugees back to Australia for medical treatment. Some of those in Australia live in the community on temporary bridging visas, but more than 200 are detained in centers.

The continued detention of asylum seekers is not only punitive and cruel, but also unlawful. Under international law, immigration detention is not a form of punishment, but rather an exceptional measure of last resort to carry out a legitimate aim. Migrants should be detained for the shortest time necessary, and only be lawfully deported if they have exhausted their remedies after full and fair asylum procedures

This situation is a stark reminder that Australia has gone from being a country that once welcomed newcomers to a world leader in treating refugees with brazen cruelty. Advocates emphasize that seven years is long enough for Australians to see the harm of offshore processing and to call on the government to end it once and for all, and to finally let refugees settle in Australia and move on with their lives.

Chapter 5

Europe: A Continent on the Move

The recent 'refugee crisis' is often bemoaned as the largest migration to Europe. However, the picture of migration on the European continent is much more complex. The refugees seeking safe haven in Europe might be currently the largest group on the move, but migration to Europe is not a new phenomenon. Additionally, intra-European mobility has also been considerable, especially since the accession of several Eastern and Central European countries in 2004.

Labor migration to Europe

Before the early nineteenth century, European governments regarded migration as a thread. They feared that migrants would disrupt the cohesion of existing states and societies. This fear resulted in comprehensive surveillance of mobility of both citizens and immigrants. However, by the end of the nineteenth century, employment levels of foreign-born workers rose considerably, especially in western and central Europe. Restrictions were tightened again as demands from the labor movements for the protection of national labor markets grew. Racism and xenophobia resulting from growing nationalistic tendencies, colonialism, and imperialism also contributed to increased restrictions on labor migration, especially in the 1880s and later on after World War I.

Fast-forward to the 1990s when the Treaty on the Functioning of the European Union created the principle of free labor mobility allowing citizens of EU member states to enter the labor markets of other member states to seek employment. As Martin Kahanec emphasizes, the free movement principle was little debated when countries at similar levels of economic development joined the EU. However, the accession to the European Union of countries with considerably lower levels of income such as the eastern enlargement to eight Central and Eastern European countries (EU-8) led to significant controversies and fears.

In 2005, French nationalists complained in the press that Polish plumbers were taking French jobs. The "Polish plumber" quickly became a shorthand across the European continent for a debate about immigration and labor. Poland responded with a tourist poster featuring a hunky model posing as a plumber whispering seductively "I am staying in Poland; won't you come over?" A similar poster was produced when Polish nurses were being recruited to work in western European countries.

These complaints were voiced at the time when western Europe experienced considerable shortages of workers in different industries. Moreover, empirical evidence did not indicate negative effects on the receiving countries' labor markets and welfare systems.

Intra-European mobility

After the fall of communist regimes in Central and Eastern Europe, many predicted that migrants from the East would arrive in Western Europe in droves. Some academics indicated that there was also a huge migration potential from the former Soviet Union. Initially, these predictions did not materialize. The millions of migrants expected to arrive from the former USSR never arrived. Forced migration from the former Yugoslavia was more substantial. However, the refugees represented only a small proportion of the millions of people driven out of their homes by armed conflict. This much smaller than expected scale of migration was directly related to restrictive immigration policies pursued by Western European countries after 1989. A *cordon sanitaire* of sorts was erected to protect Western Europe from the Commonwealth of Independent States (CIS) countries and the Balkans.

Nevertheless, in the early 1990s, considerable numbers of irregular migrants from Poland, Romania, Ukraine, Albania, and Bulgaria arrived in Western Europe. Germany, France, Britain, Belgium, Switzerland, and later also Spain, Greece, Norway, and the Netherlands set up special programs to facilitate temporary labor migration. With time, strong social networks and transnational communities developed and Central and Eastern European migrants became bolder and less risk averse.

With the May 2004 accession of new CEE member states (A8), intra-European mobility changed even further, no longer fitting traditional conceptualizations of international migration. This transformation of migration is best illustrated by mobility of Poles. For more than a century, Poland has been one of the largest migrant-sending countries in Central and Eastern Europe and a vast reservoir of labor for many states in Western Europe and North America. Poland's accession to the European Union, coupled with unrestricted entry to the United Kingdom, Sweden, and Ireland and the subsequent opening up of all EU labor markets, caused one of the biggest emigrations in the country's postwar history. On November 19, 2006, the *New York Times* reported that 800,000 Poles left the country since Poland joined the EU. The number of Polish residents who stayed abroad for at least two months tripled between early 2004 and early 2007 from approximately 180,000 to 540,000. With this exodus Poland became one of the largest exporters of labor within the enlarged European Union.

The post-accession period witnessed an intensification of short-term, circular, movements— mobility rather than migration—with Germany remaining a key destination country. Polish migrants, who for decades regarded the United States as the 'promised land' to settle in permanently, shifted their focus to Europe, much more geographically accessible and therefore not necessarily considered a place of permanent settlement. Polish migration took a form of 'pendulum' or 'circular' migration and in some cases transnational commuting. This increase of short-term movements, no longer between just two countries (in the classic transnational framework), but often to several different countries in short successions, was accompanied by a corresponding fall in permanent emigration.

Scholars termed this new mobility of Poles 'liquid migration.' Terms such as 'fluidity' and 'liquidity' are fitting metaphors when we wish to grasp the nature of the present, in many ways a *novel*, phase in the history of Polish migration or more generally international migration. Poles are now not only free to leave Poland, but also are free to leave and to come back.

Poles use their spatial mobility to adapt to the new context of post-communist space and EU enlargement. Rather than relying on transnational networking for improving their condition in the country of their settlement, many Poles tend to settle within mobility, staying mobile as long as they can in order to improve or maintain a particular quality of life, enhance their professional qualifications, and pursue educational goals. Their experience of migration becomes their lifestyle, their leaving home and going away, paradoxically, a strategy of staying at home, and, thus, an alternative to what international migration used to be considered: emigration or immigration. The liquidity of these post-socialist and post-accession population movements has received considerable academic attention, with a growing number of studies addressing the originality of these East-West movements. In terms of Polish migration, the increasing diversity of destination countries has been stressed. My own reading of this literature indicates, however, over-emphasis on macro-level processes without an in-depth understanding of the effects of mobility on individuals, families, households, and localities, including family, household, and community members left behind; the relationship between levels of mobility and life stages; and preoccupation with migration and mobility in eastern and southern Poland at the cost of excluding the analysis of mobility in and from other parts of the country.

Kathy Burrell makes two major points about this apparent explosion of mobility within Europe at the end of the twentieth century. The first, in her view, is closely tied to Anne-Marie Fortier's assertion that Europe itself can be imagined through its migration flow and that the identity of the continent is represented and reflected in the movement of bodies within it. She points out that it is tempting to link the increased freedom of movement of Eastern Europeans with the various commentaries about the 'return to Europe' of former East bloc countries. However, the gap between the rhetoric and the reality of 'returned' and 'restored' Europe is the second point that needs to be made. The divide between East and West is still clearly visible in the post-colonial discourses on the 'backwardness' of Eastern Europe and in the treatment and experiences of those testing the limits of the new Europe, inequality of mobility, and access to social services, to name just a few persisting challenges.

Gender and migration

European authorities often differentiated between migration of men and women. At the beginning of the nineteenth century, women's mobility was restricted. Some countries outright forbade migration of women. Germany, for example, did not allow women who planned to leave their children behind to migrate. Men, however, were allowed to migrate even if they planned to do the same. After World War I, several European countries continued to restrict mobility of women by refusing them passports. On the other hand, during the depression of the 1930s, European governments did not allow men to migrate, but women were free to move.

In the late twentieth and early twenty-first centuries, large number of migrants, both men and women, arrived in Italy, Greece, and Spain. Currently, there are approximately 2.2 million foreign-born residents (excluding asylum seekers) in Italy. The demand for eldercare and childcare provides opportunities for women. At the last count, a few years ago, there were 1.3 million women from Romania, Ukraine, Albania, and Morocco. Several European countries offer opportunities to women, while they restrict mobility of men. In Ireland, for instance, there are opportunities for nurses from the Philippines.

Women outnumber men in the Ukrainian, Polish, Russian, Moldovan, and Latin American communities in Italy. Women from Eastern Europe and Latin America have replaced earlier migrants from Morocco, both men and women, in Spain. Immigrant women outnumber men in Poland and Estonia, while in Hungary and Slovenia men outnumber women among emigrants.

Chapter 6

The Immigrant Experience.

Focus on Integration

The immigrant experience has always been characterized by the tension between integration into the host society and preservation of ethnic identity and cultural heritage. Some migration scholars argue that the modern phenomena of multiculturalism and transnationalism diminish incentives for immigrants to participate in their new communities. Many policy-makers claim that multiculturalism is bad precisely because it does not facilitate integration.

Policy-makers debate immigrants' experiences almost exclusively within the framework of immigrant integration. These debates do not always define what is meant by integration and how integration is measured. One often gets the feeling that policy-makers use the term 'integration,' but operationalize it as 'assimilation' and 'acculturation.' In other words, they want immigrants to become just like the 'natives.'

Migration scholars agree that it is difficult to measure integration, particularly social and cultural integration. Economic integration, on the other hand, can be measured by rates of labor force participation, job retention, wages, and length of time it takes migrants to catch up with natives in terms of earning power and economic upward mobility. In my opinion, the last element is very important because it speaks to equality and equity. While immigrants might not want to become like the 'natives' in terms of the way they socialize or what they cook, how they celebrate holidays, we all want to have the same rights that citizens of the countries where we settled have.

Oftentimes, policy-makers (over)emphasize obligations immigrants have to their new country. In fact, in some countries, immigrants must participate in integration courses and perform a number of tasks to enjoy privileges such as residency permits and access to publicly-funded services. However, for immigrants, integration is also an issue of rights, not solely of obligations.

Integration

The dominant analytical framework for immigrant integration was the great transatlantic European migration, which changed the face of the United States in the early 1900s. The political context dominated by two world wars reinforced the conceptualization of integration as a linear process of movement away from the culture and social relations of the sending country. The dominant narratives of immigrant assimilation were based on three assumptions: that a 'clean break' from the country of origin was needed before the process of integration could begin; that immigrants would eventually join the mainstream dominated by a homogenous middle-class society of European ancestry; and that this transition was inherently good for the immigrants.

Elzbieta M. Gozdziak and Susan F. Martin
Beyond the Gateway. Immigrants in a Changing America

In spite of being a country largely shaped by immigration, the United States does not have immigrant policies. No federal laws explicitly promote social, economic, or civic integration. While governments of other large immigration countries, such as Canada and Australia, have implemented policies designed to bring immigrants into the fold, newcomers have not necessarily been worse off under the U.S. system. I write this fully aware that immigrants have faced many challenges, especially under the Trump administration. Hopefully, under the Biden presidency, the country will again welcome immigrants and continue to protect them to the best of our ability.

Without officially endorsing multiculturalism, the way Canada does, the U.S. government has developed a legal framework that nevertheless protects newcomers and guarantees a broad array of rights. Several policies protect both citizens and immigrants from discrimination on the basis of race, religion, nationality, and, in some cases, citizenship. Prior to the Trump administration, employers, for example, had been penalized for refusing to hire a foreign-sounding or foreign-looking person on suspicion that the applicant does not have appropriate documentation. These laws did not end prejudice, but they provided solid footing for immigrants to defend their rights.

The private sector had also taken a lead role in promoting integration in the United States. Family members and employers sponsor immigrants and take principal responsibility for ensuring their successful adaptation to their new country. A flexible labor market has facilitated the efforts of immigrant advocates by making employment easy to find. Although many jobs do not pay well and often do not offer many benefits, it is possible for immigrants to improve their lot and even own their own businesses.

Given their high levels of employment, immigrants, both documented and undocumented, are frequently characterized as hard-working contributors to the nation's economy, which also eases the integration process.

Several broad and long-standing government policies aid integration indirectly. Among the most important is birthright citizenship, granted automatically to children of immigrants if they are born on U.S. territory. The provision applies even to children of undocumented migrants. As a result, only one generation carries the label of 'foreigner,' in contrast to many European countries where children and grandchildren of immigrants grow up in migrancy. Migrancy is not simply a condition of being a migrant, but rather a socially constructed subjectivity which is inscribed on black and brown bodies by the larger society as well as legislative practices. Often migrancy is not only attributed to those who have migrated, but also to children and grandchildren of immigrants, children who have never moved away from their place of birth.

When riots broke out in several cities in France in November 2005, people were asking who the rioters were. Many were children and grandchildren of non-European immigrants. They were born in France, had French citizenship and French passports, but the French still called them 'immigrants.' As French citizens, they shared the same rights and protections accorded all French citizens, at least that is what is said on paper. In reality, many were as alienated from their parents and their ethnic roots as they were from mainstream French society, which objects to "positive discrimination," or affirmative action, and does not want to recognize the diversity existing in France. The French are not alone. 'Immigrants' in Germany, the Netherlands, Italy and elsewhere in Europe are equally disenfranchised. The different models of immigrant integration tested in Europe, including the by now discredited 'guest worker' approach followed for years by Germany and Austria, and the path to blended Europe taken by Britain and France, have failed. But why did they fail? The simple and not necessarily simplistic answer is because many European states followed a top-down approach, which called for national integration policies without empowering immigrants and the second generation to make decisions at the local level and wage the challenge of integration from the bottom-up. Only in 2003 did the French government encourage the formation of an umbrella Islamic organization that could represent French Muslims in a dialogue with the state. But then again, this just affords representation at the state level. Only anger and matches were left at the local level.

The U.S. policies, as imperfect as they have been, have always reflected a deep-rooted national conviction that immigration is good for the country and immigrants are its future. The basic framework for naturalization dates to the early nineteenth century and the ideas of the founding fathers. The founding fathers saw immigrants as presumptive citizens who should enjoy the same rights and privileges as other Americans.

In contrast to the birthright citizenship, almost all states in Europe, Asia, Africa, and Oceania grant citizenship at birth based upon the principle of *jus sanguinis* (right of blood), in which citizenship is inherited through parents rather than birthplace, or a restricted version of *jus soli* in which citizenship by birthplace is automatic only for the children of certain immigrants. Interestingly, in many countries, children born to a native and a foreign parent, are considered citizens of the foreign-born parent's country, not the country where the native parent and they were born. While children of immigrants may be considered Americans from the day they are born, economic, cultural and political integration takes place over the span of many generations. Like the children of immigrants who came decades ago, those who arrived in the most recent wave of migration see themselves as Americans and will almost certainly integrate more easily than their parents. But that is not to say they will achieve equal footing with their counterparts born to established residents. Integration does not happen overnight.

In the traditional immigration countries, time and the overarching policy framework both indirectly favor integration, but neither is a substitute for action at the community level, where the web of local relationships determines the immigrant experience. In the United States, one consequence of the federal government's hands-off approach to integration is an even greater reliance on communities and community leadership, including ethnic community leadership. Experiences at local levels shape not only immigrant attitudes toward their new country but also the cohesiveness of the neighborhoods, towns, and cities they adopt as their new homes. My own research in several new settlement areas in the United States has demonstrated that local actors, including the newcomers themselves, have found novel ways to assume this responsibility and foster the incorporation of newly arrived immigrants into broader society.

The dynamics of integration, of course, cannot be reduced to a negotiation between two groups. A categorization of two camps such as 'established residents' and 'newcomers' classifies individuals according only to when they arrived and does not account for infinite social divisions along ethnic, racial, and religious lines. The host societies in many countries are composed of different waves of newcomers, some more empathetic than others to the newest arrivals. Today's immigrant population is also comprised of several subcategories. In the United States, newcomers with refugee status benefit from generous U.S. assistance programs that can become a source of tension with other immigrants. In some cases, long-standing ethnic divisions are renewed in the settlement country, as illustrated by tribal rivalries among Somali immigrants in the United States. This complexity means that immigrants arrive to find a country more diverse than the lands they leave behind. Integration becomes a multipronged process, with newcomers finding their way among the many segments of mainstream society and other immigrant communities.

Research in different parts of the world indicates that many common obstacles to social, economic, and civic integration exist. While some of these challenges might be remedied with more effective policies, many of them also derive from cultural rifts that call for nothing less than changes in the perceptions that established residents, including earlier immigrants, and newcomers have of each other. Bridging the gaps that separate these different groups would strengthen communities, mitigate divisive social tensions, and, of course, position immigrants to participate more effectively in the wider society.

One obstacle that arises is a perception that labor migrants, for example, will leave as soon as they make enough money, thereby making it unnecessary to include them in broad society. Of course, some migrants move on --we call it secondary migration— but most stay in the same place if they feel welcomed. In the United States, the perception that immigrants comprised a transient population was transformed in some cases into a denial of responsibility for Latino health care, education, housing, and retirement needs. Germans were surprised that when they invited guest workers, they got people who wanted to settle and bring family members.

The exclusion of immigrants from conceptions of local communities, beyond contributing to their marginalization, can also lead to depictions of newcomers as liabilities. Particularly amid economic difficulties, immigrants perceived as lacking other links to a community are frequently seen to take advantage of support networks or, worse yet, take jobs that would otherwise go to established residents. On the other hand, during the current pandemic, we see many immigrants as essential workers without whom harvest would not be completed, groceries and other necessities would not be delivered. Some countries recognize the contributions immigrants have made to fighting COVID-19. France has recognized these contributions and is planning to award front line medical personnel French citizenship.

In many countries, much of the opposition to migration stems from the widespread belief that the majority of migrants are illegal or irregular migrants, even though the opposite is usually the case. In the United States, when policy-makers seek to restrict benefits for undocumented immigrants, their decisions frequently affect family members who may be refugees or children who are U.S. citizens. At community levels, many programs and publications further complicate the issue by using definitions of immigrants that do not correspond with individuals' legal status. Examples include the designation of African-born children as 'African Americans' in school data and counts of individuals who identify as Latinos, but were born in the United States.

The news media significantly influence the popular perception of immigrants, reinforcing stereotypes in some cases while empathizing with the foreigner's experience in others. I have seen this happening on both sides of the Atlantic. The arrival of large numbers of asylum seekers in Europe, starting in 2015, has attracted substantial news coverage, magnifying their presence. Newcomer status, perceived or real, frequently influences the tone of the media's treatment. Asylum seekers arriving in Europe as well as those arriving at the U.S.-Mexico border have been portrayed as illegal arrivals or even criminal aliens. Regrettably, coverage of immigrant issues frequently concentrates on moments of conflict between natives and newcomers. In the aftermath of terrorist attacks, media outlets have been more likely to cast newcomers in a menacing light even if the terrorists were home-grown.

A common challenge is to emphasize the contributions made by immigrants, encouraging their acceptance as full-fledged members of the community and promoting tolerance. Whether focused on economic or social aspects, successful integration programs have generally helped established residents to acknowledge that immigrants bring something of value. In the United States, beyond labor, immigrant contributions highlighted by advocates have included economic investment, cultural diversity, and the resuscitation of depopulated urban and rural areas.

By the same token, integration depends on the empowerment of immigrants for participation in the wider community. In both social and economic terms, it is important to stress opportunities and obligations as much as rights and entitlements. One of the largest obstacles to this goal is that mediating institutions such as schools, hospitals, and

local governments often overlook the newcomer voice. This condition owes largely to immigrants' lack of familiarity with their new communities. Links of incorporation within newcomer groups and with broad society remedy this condition over time, but several smaller initiatives—sports tournaments, festivals, cultural heritage preservation programs-- have potential to accelerate this orientation.

Much as the benefits of immigration must be realized, integration also requires an honest and clear assessment of the problems faced by newcomers. To ignore the costs of immigration—whether the fiscal costs to institutions unused to providing services to clients with limited proficiency in the dominant or official language, or the social costs when immigrants knowingly or inadvertently break laws or violate community norms—is to jeopardize the future integration of immigrants.

Economically, opportunities for upward mobility represent a crucial incentive for newcomers to integrate themselves. Investment and professional advancement beyond ethnic businesses not only promote linkages with the host society but also help newcomers build foundations for their children. Some migration scholars have concluded that these opportunities are unlikely to be extended by the host community and depend on the organization of immigrants to demand fair treatment. Even when the established business community does seek to incorporate newcomers, language and cultural barriers make it difficult to connect.

Whatever the level of integration, one pivotal task is to ensure that newcomers are not disenfranchised. Low graduation rates among immigrant high school students reflect a failure of integration efforts to date. By limiting the number of bilingual role models in public schools, the trend also promotes a vicious cycle and increases the likelihood of greater challenges in the future. The role models must also include teachers and school administrators. I am always amazed when my European colleagues visiting public schools in the United States remark that foreign-born teachers who speak with an accent should not be allowed to teach. Why? By this token, I should not be a college professor as I too speak with an accent.

In the context of the 'war on terror,' warnings against disenfranchisement of newcomers have taken on new resonance. In the United States, detentions of foreign-born residents are a high-profile example of what many have called a widespread erosion of immigrants' civil liberties. Raids targeting undocumented workers at transportation hubs and other workplaces, for example, have elicited protests and heightened social tensions. Although most newcomers are not suspected of criminal intentions, federal officials have argued that immigrants without the proper documents could become victims of extortion by international terrorists. Perceptions of antagonism nevertheless might make newcomers more reluctant to embrace and participate in their new communities.

At the most basic level, a culture of exchange among newcomers and established communities depends on establishing a baseline level of trust. Ideally, newcomers would receive a thorough orientation to the social mores, laws, and legal systems of their new country. For better or worse, law enforcement authorities become one of the most visible points of contact, setting a tone for wider community relations in their interactions with immigrants. Too often, police lack the resources to communicate with immigrants, who frequently distrust law enforcement because of experiences in their homelands. A focus on immigration status, rather than a holistic approach that also views newcomers as potential victims and witnesses, can further antagonize relations.

For all the efforts by host communities to facilitate integration, newcomers take charge of their own lives soon after their arrival. As they negotiate their own transition from newcomers to established residents, their success depends in part on the degree to which they coordinate their efforts with one another. Just as immigrants maximize their power vis-a`-vis broader society by articulating common political and economic interests, they improve their own prospects in integration by asserting themselves with one voice. A united front is most crucial in nation-states where cultural or religious homogeneity marginalizes outsiders, but all newcomer communities benefit from coordinating the efforts of internal subgroups and advocates. Such efforts allow newcomer groups to pursue their objectives more effectively, improve communication with the host society, and create political space that will benefit future generations.

Chapter 7

Diasporas and Transnational Communities

In the past couple of decades, the concepts of diaspora and transnational communities have been used as powerful lenses through which to study international migration and debate the policy ramifications of diasporic and transnational communities and processes. Both concepts are complex and contested. It is impossible to do justice to this complexity in a short book and present all the contestations. I will therefore focus on several issues I find most intriguing and worthy of debate.

Diaspora

The term 'diaspora' can be found everywhere: in academic literature, in policy debates at the World Bank, and in works of fiction. There is even a whole journal devoted to diaspora studies. The term and the concept have become household words and have been enlisted in the services of various intellectual, cultural, political, and economic agendas.

It is not a new term. As Stéphane Dufoix writes, in its original meaning the concept of diaspora did not indicate a historical dispersal such as the Babylonian exile of Jews in the sixth century BCE. Rather, it described divine punishment—the dispersal throughout the world—that would befall the Jews if they did not obey God's commandments. As such the word referred to a theological rather than a historical dispersal. In this conceptualization the dispersal as well as the return of the dispersed is a matter of divine, not human, will. In the New Testament, the word diaspora is used to refer to members of the Christian church being exiled from the City of God and dispersed across the Earth. The condition of this dispersion was understood as the proof of them being the Chosen People.

Today, the term is used to describe those who identify with a 'homeland,' but live outside its borders. Gabriel Sheffer in *Modern Diasporas in International Politics* defines modern diasporas as ethnic minority groups of migrant origins residing and acting in host countries, but maintaining strong sentimental and material links with their countries of origin. Despite criticisms that the concept may suggest homogeneity and a historically fixed identity, as well as shared values and practices, diasporas are celebrated by academics, community leaders, and policy-makers.

Michel Bruneau uses four essential criteria to identify diasporas. First, the population has to be dispersed under pressure—disaster, catastrophe, famine, abject poverty-- in several places, not immediately neighboring the territory of origin. Second, the choice of countries and cities of destination is carried out in accordance with the structure of migratory chains, which link migrants with those already settled in the host countries. Third, this population is integrated without being assimilated in the host countries. Members of a diaspora retain strong identity awareness linked to the memory of the territory, of the society of origin, and its history. Fourth, these dispersed groups of migrants preserve and develop among them and with the society of origin, multiple exchange relations organized under networks. Relations tend to be horizontal rather than vertical.

In Bruneau's conceptualization, in order to transmit its identity from one generation to the next, a diaspora must have places for religious, cultural, and political gatherings. These can be sanctuaries (churches, synagogues, mosques, etc.), community premises (conference rooms, theatres, libraries, sports clubs, etc.), or monuments that can be used for commemorations. Bruneau includes also restaurants and grocery shops, newsagents and the media. These various places can be concentrated in the same "ethnic" neighborhood or be dispersed throughout a city or a larger territory.

Four major types of diasporas stem from these four criteria. The first set of diasporas—the Chinese, Indian, and Lebanese diasporas, for example—center around entrepreneurship as the main element of the reproduction strategy. The second set of diasporas centers around religion, often linked to a language, as the main structuring element. The Jewish, Greek, Armenian, and Assyro-Chaldean diasporas are given as examples. The religion is monotheistic and strongly connected to a sacred language, be it Hebrew, Greek, Aramaic, or Armenian. Bruneau argues that enterprises play a very important role in the life of Jewish, Greek, and Armenian diasporas, but they are not the central feature that ensures the reproduction of the diaspora in the long run. That central element is religion: the synagogue and the church, with a pronounced ethnic tint, are the constitutive elements of these diaspora communities. The third set of diasporas is organized primarily around politics. Bruneau uses the Palestinian diaspora as an example here. He posits that when the territory of origin is dominated by a foreign power, the main aspiration of the population of the diaspora is political. The diaspora aims to create a nation-state. He cites the example of the Palestinian diaspora, which had succeeded in establishing a real state in exile, the Palestinian Liberation Organization (PLO), whose objective was to establish a nation-state next to the state of Israel. The fourth set is centered on race and culture as in the case of the Black diaspora. This diaspora has no direct affiliation with the societies or territories of origin.

It is interesting that Bruneau does not include wars or other forms of armed conflict as criteria for dispersal. This typology excludes forced migrants—refugees and asylum seekers—as well as dissidents expelled from their countries of origin. The focus on migratory chains also excludes newcomers who settle in countries with no history of migration of members of their group. The taxonomy, while elegant, does not reflect the complexity of diasporic communities.

In my experience, many, but not all, immigrants who identify with their countries of origin also identify with a particular diaspora. One only needs to look at research on Mexican hometown associations to see the strong two-way links. These associations are based on the social networks that migrants from the same town or village in Mexico establish in their new U.S. communities. Members of these associations, commonly known as *clubes de oriundos*, seek to promote the well-being of their hometown communities of both origin (in Mexico) and residence (in the U.S.) by raising money to fund public works and social projects. Many African immigrants identify not just with their home country, but with the continent and form pan-African networks. When allowed by local legislation, members of some diasporas run for public offices in their countries of origin, often bringing back social and political remittances acquired while living outside the boundaries of their home countries.

While the concept of diaspora is often contested, some immigrants prefer to use this concept and associated term to describe themselves and their community organizations. Recalling his research in the African communities in London, Khalid Koser found that the preference for the term 'diaspora' stemmed from the fact that African immigrants thought there were fewer negative connotations associated with the term diaspora than with the terms 'immigrant,' 'refugee,' or 'asylum seeker.'

However, for many immigrants the relationship to the diaspora is not as straightforward and not very positive. Whether one identifies with a particular diaspora or not is often very much a political statement. Known as *Polonia*, the Polish diaspora includes Poles and people of Polish heritage or origin who live outside Poland. The Polish Ministry of Foreign Affairs estimates the size of the Polish diaspora at 18-20 million. The largest Polish diasporas are in the United States (approximately 9.6 million according to 2012 reports), in Germany (1.5 million), and in Canada (1 million). This makes *Polonia* one of the largest diasporas in the world and one of the most widely dispersed. However, only one-third of the members of the Polish diaspora were born in Poland. The ties the second and third generation of Polish Americans, for example, have to the ancestral homeland are often very tangential and superficial. Many of the very mobile Poles living and working in the European Union since the accession in 2004 do not even identify as immigrants. They speak of moving abroad or studying in a foreign country, but not so much about settlement and emigration. This is true especially in relation to movement within the European Union.

In my recent research of Polish women living and working in Norway, my interlocutors did not necessarily discuss their move in terms of migration or permanency. Most women spoke about 'moving to Norway' or 'coming to Norway.' Many described their situation as 'living in Norway.' Few identified as immigrants. Why would they? When a French woman moves to Berlin for a new job, her move is labelled 'job transfer.' Nevertheless, many policy makers consider Poles migrants. The European Commission, for example, regards Italians living in Barcelona as 'mobile citizens' or 'free movers,' but they consider citizens of the A8 countries, i.e., citizens of the 2004 enlargement countries, as 'migrants' since in the eyes of the receiving countries their integration seems problematic.

Not all Polish emigrants identify with the Polish diaspora. My own research dating back to the mid-

1980s in several metropolitan areas in the United States where large numbers of Poles lived indicated a great deal of diversity, in many ways mirroring the social strata of Polish society in Poland, in terms of educational backgrounds, types of professions, and ability to speak English. I found considerable differences between resettlement experiences of Polish immigrants in cities such as Chicago and New York that have had a long history of Polish immigration and cities such as Dallas, Texas, Washington, D.C. or Atlanta, Georgia that had virtually no Polish population before the 1980s. There are no Polish neighborhoods in Washington, D.C., Dallas or Atlanta. While the Roman Catholic Church of Our Lady Queen of Poland in Silver Spring, Maryland has served as a center of worship for some Polish immigrants, only a handful of Polish families live in that neighborhood. There is always a crowd of Poles—nostalgic for the pageantry of the Corpus Christi procession, anxious to have their Easter eggs blessed on Holy Saturday, and ready to sing Christmas carols during midnight mass on Christmas Eve—at the church on major holy days. Many, particularly members of Polish intelligentsia, prefer more liberal American Catholic churches such as Holy Trinity in Georgetown or St. John's in Silver Spring. Most Polish families are dispersed throughout northern Virginia and Maryland suburbs. A few families reside in the District of Columbia, but the Poles settled in the Washington metropolitan area are invisible. The only time one hears Polish spoken on the streets of Washington is when a renowned Polish symphony orchestra plays at the Kennedy Center or when Poles flock to the Polish Embassy to cast their absentee ballots during a parliamentary or presidential election.

Poles living abroad—whether in North America or in Europe-- are also quite divided politically. During the most recent presidential election, progressive Poles living in Poland argued that Poles living abroad should not be allowed to vote in Polish elections as many are very conservative and support the Law and Order (PiS) party. The criticism was aimed primarily at Poles who have been living abroad for many years and have no intention of returning to Poland, not at economic migrants staying outside the borders of Poland on a temporary basis. In other words, the blame targeted the old Polonia, not the new mobile members of Polish society.

Mary Patrice Erdmans, who has done a lot of research with and among Poles and Polish Americans (my distinction), especially in Chicago, has raised some interesting questions regarding the conceptualization of diaspora and ethnic identity. In her book *Opposite Poles*, Erdmans provides a dramatic account of intracommunity conflict in Chicago and demonstrates the importance of distinguishing between immigrants and ethnics in American ethnic studies. Her research shows that while common ancestral heritage creates the potential for ethnic allegiance, it is not a sufficient condition for collective action. John Bukowczyk also wonders how the Polish diaspora is made. Polish governments, even during the communist era, have always thought of Polonia as a rather homogenous community dispersed around the world but united by common blood ties. This is a very primordial way of conceptualizing the Polish diaspora and Polish identity. In the eyes of the Polish government, my daughter, born in Washington D.C. to a card-carrying Polish mother and an Irish American father, will always be considered Polish and have Polish citizenship despite the fact that she does not speak a word of Polish. I consider her an American, but the Polish government claims her as a Polish citizen.

In my experience, members of the Polish diaspora might be willing to open businesses in Poland, but I have not encountered people who want to send remittances to support public projects. The Great Orchestra of Christmas Charity (Wielka Orkiestra Świątecznej Pomocy, WOŚP), the biggest non-governmental charity in Poland raising money for pediatric and elderly care, had not tapped into the Polish diaspora until 2019 when they set up a PayPal account. I am not sure how much money they managed to collect.

On the other hand, members of many diasporas actively support humanitarian and development initiatives. In the aftermath of the 2010 earthquake in Haiti, the Haitian diaspora served as an invaluable conduit for Creole-speaking doctors, nurses, engineers, educators, advisers, and reconstruction planners. Haitian-Americans continued to be vital in long-term recovery and rebuilding in Haiti through remittances, sharing human and financial resources, lobbying governments, international organizations, and corporations for disaster-relief and redevelopment funding, supplies, and eased travel restrictions. Examining the role of the Nepali migrant and diaspora population living in the United States after the 2015 earthquake, Richa Shivakoti noted their active involvement in sending remittances to their families and towards relief efforts, but also emphasized a strong trust deficit among the Nepali diaspora in the U.S. and agencies related to the Nepali government.

International organizations such as the World Bank and the International Organization for Migration (IOM) and even research outfits such as the International Centre for Migration Policy Development (ICMPD) actively encourage diaspora communities to support development in their respective countries of origin. I have always wondered whether policy makers ever stop to think about the effects of remittances on immigrants' integration in settlement countries. While some immigrants can afford to support development projects in countries of origin and many do, equally many live very precarious lives and struggle to make ends meet and integrate both economically and socially in the settlement countries. Thinking about these complex issues, I am often reminded of research on gendered ways of immigrant economic behaviors. In one study, the researchers found that female migrants from the Dominican Republic living in New York City spent money on kitchen appliances to ease their housework and invested in their children's education while their husbands sent money to support projects in the Dominican Republic and engaged in political causes.

Transnational communities

A concept closely related to diaspora is that of 'transnational communities.' Transnational community often refers to those migrants who reside in a receiving nation for a considerable period of time yet maintain strong transnational ties. Those ties may be reinforced formally by the rules and regulations of the state (immigration laws, definitions of citizenship), by links with political parties or religious groups, or informally through connections among families and households in the sending and receiving countries.

As developed nations became more economically dependent on the immigrant labor force, there was more political pressure for the state to enter reciprocal relationships with those groups, particularly those of long-term residence. For example, until 2000 the rules and regulations for defining and obtaining German citizenship excluded the large Turkish population residing in the country for many decades. The Turks living in Germany desired dual citizenship. They defined citizenship in terms of political representation and nationality, but wanted to preserve their ethnic identity. This goal conflicted with the German definition of citizenship, which combined citizenship with nationality. The Turkish minority was rooted in a Turkish national identity and a Muslim religious identity, both foreign to the German collective identity, yet Germany was in many ways economically dependent on that minority. Pressure for change resulted in the reform of Germany's citizenship and nationality law in 2000.

In her ethnography *The Transnational Villagers*, Peggy Levitt emphasizes that many migrants and those that never migrated engage in different transnational activities, but not all are embedded in transnational social fields, nor do all belong to transnational communities. She distinguishes individuals who travel regularly to conduct routine economic and political activities; those whose lives are rooted in a single place although much of what they do involves resources, contacts, and people in the country of origin; and those who do not move but who live their lives within a transnational context. Levitt proceeds to provide examples of transnational migrants. She mentions entrepreneurs who traverse borders to obtain money, information, and supplies; political party officials whose job is to coordinate activities between the United States and the home country; parents who leave children behind to be cared for by grandparents or other family members; and individuals who never migrated but who are dependent on the economic remittances they receive monthly and who live in a socio-cultural context completely transformed by migration.

While modern technological advances aid formation of transnational communities, living transnationally is not new. Nancy Foner reminds us that between 1910 and 1920, for every 100 immigrants who entered the United States, a little more than one-third returned. Between 1880 and 1930, an estimated one-quarter to one-third of all immigrants to America repatriated. Remitting money to one's relatives in the homeland is also nothing new. Immigrants also supported improvement projects back home. Between 1910 and 1920, Italian immigrants remitted so much money that the Society for the Protection of Italian Immigrants claimed that Italians in New York contributed more to the tax rolls in Italy than taxpayers in the poor provinces of Sicily and Calabria.

Despite similarities, there are also differences between transnational communities of the past and the present. There is a difference in scale. While nearly one-quarter of the Irish population migrated in the 1920s, Polish and Italian immigrants to the United States constituted barely four percent of the population, each. In the early 2000s, the proportion of migrants leaving sending countries reached double-digits. Communication technology enables members of transnational communities to stay in touch with family members in the home country on a daily basis. Many grandmothers in Poland read bedtime stories to their grandchildren living in Norway or the United Kingdom every night. Children left behind communicate with parents daily as well. Despite all the criticism of Polish parents who went to the UK or Ireland after the accession to the European Union in 2004, many teens I interviewed told me they had better and closer relationships with their parents, fathers especially, aided by Skype and WhatsApp, after their parents migrated than when they were in Poland working two or three jobs to make ends meet.

Another difference I noted was that transnational communities do not necessarily span just two countries. Often times, members of the same family are scattered across several borders. Transnational mobility also affects how migrants define 'home.' In *Moving Matters*, Susan Ossman paints a portrait of the serial migrant: a person who has lived in several countries, calling each one at some point 'home.' The stories that the book tells are both extraordinary and increasingly common. Serial migrants rarely travel freely—they must negotiate a world of territorial borders and legal restrictions—yet as they move from one country to another, they can use border-crossings as moments of self-clarification. They often become masters of settlement as they turn each country into a life chapter. Ossman follows this diverse and growing population not only to understand how paths of serial movement produce certain ways of life, but also to illuminate an ongoing tension between global fluidity and the power of nation-states.

I have a feeling that as mobility evolves, we will revisit the conceptualizations of diasporic and transnational communities to make sure that migration scholarship catches up and properly reflects the rich and nuanced processes and communities.

Chapter 8

Securitization of Migration

Speaking from the Oval Office in the White House on January 8, 2019, Donald Trump warned the American people that if the U.S.-Mexican border is not secured and a wall is not erected, drugs, criminals, and terrorists will continue pouring into the country and will jeopardize the national security of the United States. Fact-checkers quickly reminded Mr. Trump that there was no credible evidence indicating that international terrorist groups have established bases in Mexico, worked with Mexican drug cartels, or sent operatives via Mexico into the United States. Data gathered by the U.S. Department of Homeland Security (DHS) further indicated that the majority of individuals on the terrorist watch list attempted to enter the United States by air. Most of the 2,554 people on the watch list encountered by U.S. officials in 2017 tried to enter through airports (2,170) or by sea (49).

These assurances did not prevent Donald Trump from continuing to argue that terrorists and criminals cross the southern border with impunity. He called El Salvador, Haiti, and a myriad of African states 'shithole countries' and banned travel from several Muslim majority countries. The U.S. Supreme Court, in a 5-4 ruling, upheld the ban. Mr. Trump also said that immigrants in the country illegally are responsible for tens of thousands of crimes, although his former Chief of Staff, John Kelly, in an interview with National Public Radio (NPR), acknowledged that most people crossing the border illegally do not pose a security threat.

Donald Trump is not the first U.S. president that has connected international migration with national security. In the aftermath of the terrorist attacks on the United States on September 11, 2001, President George W. Bush connected international migration with the need to protect the nation. Indeed, once it was announced that the nineteen hijackers were foreign nationals, those critical of the U.S. immigration system argued that the government must use all available means to protect the national security of the country. Within a few days, the Immigration and Nationality Act (INA) was adopted and a series of reforms aimed at implementing immigration restrictions, including detention of foreign-born individuals without charge, began. On December 16, 2002, President Bush signed the National Security Directive 22, which specifically linked irregular migration and human trafficking to terrorist threats. Two years later, the U.S. Congress passed the Intelligence Reform and Terrorism Prevention Act of 2004, which established the Human Smuggling and Trafficking Center, composed of experts from the prosecutorial, law enforcement, consular, policy, intelligence, and diplomatic areas, to study the nexus of irregular migration, especially smuggling and human trafficking, and the criminal support of underground terrorist travel. Additionally, the Trafficking Victims Protection Reauthorization Act (TVPRA) of 2005 created an interagency task force with a mandate to explore the relationships between trafficking in persons and terrorism.

In parallel developments, on September 20, 2001, the Council of the European Union called for strengthening of surveillance measures, including vigilance in issuing residency permits and systematic checking of identity papers, under article 2.3 of the Schengen Convention. The bombings of Madrid on March 11, 2004, and London on July 7, 2005, further consolidated the national security policies in Europe. However, terrorist attacks on European cities— Brussels and Paris—continued. Most of the identified terrorists were Belgian or French citizens, not recent immigrants. Facts notwithstanding, policy-makers on both sides of the Atlantic allege that irregular migration, human smuggling, and human trafficking are a conduit for international terrorism

Donald J. Trump and George W. Bush are also not the only world leaders who claimed that migration, especially irregular migration, is a security threat. Viktor Orbán, the Prime Minister of Hungary, used the same argument to reject refugees fleeing conflicts in the Middle East and to build his own Fortress Hungary. Jarosław Kaczyński, the current leader of the Peace and Justice Party (PiS) in Poland, also linked migration with insecurity and a threat to 'Christian Europe'. The list of politicians presenting similar arguments is long.

Immigrants are not only seen as potential terrorists or criminals threatening national security and perpetrating dangerous crimes, they are also regarded as a threat to national identity and social cohesion. The current 'refugee crisis' in Europe has resulted in public discussions about the threat that Muslim refugees pose to the Christian identity of the continent. The debates are especially fervent in the new accession countries in Central Europe.

However, these anti-immigrant sentiments and conceptualizations of migrants as criminals and terrorists and irregular migration as trafficking predate the terrorist attacks by at least a decade or more. In the 1990s, conservative discourses identified multiculturalism as a cause of societal disintegration. The best-known version of this kind of discourse is Samuel Huntington's *The Clash of Civilizations* (1996). It mediates the differentiation between us and them by identifying other peoples and cultures that endanger the survival of the home culture. Migration is identified as being one of the main elements weakening national tradition and threatening societal homogeneity.

Unfortunately, securitization of migrants and migration is nothing new. Germans residing in the United Kingdom during World War II were interned on the grounds that they may have been 'fifth columnists.' In the United States, some 120,000 Japanese Americans were forcibly relocated and placed in concentration camps during WWII despite the fact that approximately 62 percent were U.S. citizens. Canada followed suit, relocating 21,000 of its Japanese residents. During the 1970s and 1980s Kurdish and Algerian diasporas were linked to terrorist attacks in Western Europe.

The 'refugee crisis' in Europe and elsewhere in the world has also affected the discourse at the nexus of international migration and security. Each terrorist attack spurred calls for enhanced border security, stricter visa requirements, enhanced vetting of refugees and asylum seekers, greater vigilance in issuing residency permits, and systematic checking of identity papers. As already noted, securitization of migrants and migration is not a new phenomenon. If populist attitudes are allowed to flourish, we might see even more emphasis on security.

Whom does the focus on migration and security help? Research indicates that it does not help migrants. 'Rescued' migrants are often sent back to the country that they wanted to escape. When they are allowed to stay in the destination country, the permission to stay rarely includes long-term immigration relief with the accompanying rights that legal immigrants have. Many researchers emphasize the fact that the focus on crime and security overshadows the role of the state as a protector of human rights. Does it help native-born citizens? My current research on norms and values and the 'refugee crisis' as well as my previous studies on attitudes towards migrants in Europe, suggest that criminalizing migrants and migration fosters xenophobia but doesn't necessarily prevent human trafficking, smuggling, and any other irregular migration.

Future Challenges

Many challenges remain. These challenges differ considerably depending on a country or geographic region. However, there are also many challenges different continents and countries share. These can be summarized, at minimum, as: access to the territory, asylum procedures, reception conditions, and integration.

In Europe, temporary controls within the Schengen area are still in place, at least for some sections of the Austrian, Danish, French, German, and Swedish borders. Hungary recruited 3,000 'border hunters' to join the 10,000 police and soldiers already patrolling the border, parts of which have been electrified and deliver small electric shocks to migrants. The 'smart technology' fence is also armed with heat sensors, cameras, and loudspeakers that blare warnings, in several languages, to not cross the border.

Unlike Hungary, Poland has not built a fence along its borders. However, border guards at some border crossings continuously refuse entry to persons wishing to apply for international protection. The border crossing in Brześć-Terespol on the Polish-Byelorussian border has been a main entry point for Chechens, Tajiks, and others from the post-Soviet region for many years. In 2016 alone, some 85,000 asylum seekers attempted to enter Poland in the hopes to reach the EU territory, but most were pushed back. The pushbacks constitute de facto *refoulement*, despite the fact that the principle of *non-refoulement* is the cornerstone of refugee protection enshrined in the 1951 Refugee Convention and the 1967 Protocol, both of which Poland acceded to in 1991. The European Court of Human Rights (ECHR) ordered interim measures that asylum seekers should not be refused entry at the Terespol and Medyka border crossings, but border guards disregarded these directives.

Human Rights Watch reported in 2017 that in one month in 2016 as many as 3,000 asylum seekers and migrants were turned back and stranded in Brześć. In the same year, Poland's recognition rate for asylum seekers from Russia (including Chechens) was 5.6 percent and for those from Tajikistan, 10.5 percent. This compares with an average across the EU 27 member states of 19 percent for asylum seekers from Russia and 27.5 percent for those from Tajikistan. Except for the European Court of Human Rights (ECHR), the pushbacks and the high rates of asylum application rejections met with little protest from European leaders, who have their own interests in keeping the bloc's eastern border shut.

Elsewhere in Europe, the situation is not markedly better. Non-governmental organizations (NGOs) deploying rescue vessels in the Mediterranean faced pressure from authorities to abstain from providing assistance. Migrants reaching the Italian-French border were either returned to Italy without a formal decision or detained in France without receiving information about their rights or the opportunity to apply for protection. According to some reports, as many as 95 percent of migrants apprehended at the border were returned to Italy.

Additionally, assistance to refugees is being criminalized. Hungary is the biggest offender. In June of 2018, the Hungarian Parliament approved the 'Stop Soros' bill that criminalizes assistance to undocumented migrants and creates a parallel court system to try those who attempt to assist migrants. This new legislation is accelerating efforts by Prime Minister Viktor Orbán to transform the country into what he calls an 'illiberal democracy.'

There are other examples of what advocates call criminalization of solidarity. In 2017, Cédric Herrou, an olive farmer and activist, was convicted of aiding illegal immigrants in France and fined 30,000 euros. After a prolonged legal battle, the French Constitutional Council absolved him in July 2018, but Herrou remains under constant police surveillance. Benoit Duclois, a French mountain guide, was charged for assisting a pregnant Nigerian migrant to cross the snowy Italian-French border on foot. Carola Rackete, a German captain, was arrested after forcing her way into the Sicilian port of Lampedusa on the Sea-Watch-3 carrying 40 migrants and refugees she had rescued off Libya. She was subsequently released; judge Alessandra Vella ruled that Rackete had been carrying out her duty to protect life and had not committed any acts of violence. There are many more examples of criminalizing the actions of Good Samaritans standing in solidarity with refugees.

With the launch of the *New Pact on Migration and Asylum*, the European Commission proposed to overhaul the European Union's long-ailing migration and asylum policies. Describing the pact, the European Union Vice President Margaritis Schinas used a metaphor of a three-storied building. She called the first floor the external dimension centered around strengthened partnerships with countries of origin and transit. She described the role of the second floor as robust management of external borders, and finally, the third floor she related to firm but fair internal rules. Following the metaphor of a building, some commentators wrote that the pact needs a foundational basement, in the form of recognizing that an overwhelming majority of the world's refugees are hosted in developing countries. Without a basement, the whole edifice is undermined.

They also stressed that the EU must incorporate policy ideas from the Global Compact on Refugees (GCR) to rectify this. To be honest, when the launch of the pact was first discussed, I was wondering why there was even a need for a new pact since many countries, including European countries, just signed the Global Compact on Refugees. In fact, two global compacts: one on refugees and one on migration.

Before seeing the new pact, I thought that perhaps the authors of the new pact agreed with

James Hathaway, who called the Global Compact on Refugees a Global Cop-out on Refugees. Even before he published his piece in the *International Journal of Refugee Law* and his ECRE op-ed, he said at the last conference of the International Association for the Study of Forced Migration (IASFM) in Thessaloniki that the Compact will result in lots of meetings to chat about how best to respond to 'large' refugee movements: we will have a periodic Global Refugee Forum; high-level officials' meetings between forums; meetings of national steering groups; support platforms; solidarity conferences; and regional consultative mechanisms. In other words, it will all be about process – a bureaucrat's dream, he called it, but nothing that comes even close to dependably addressing the operational deficits of the refugee regime. Many at the conference supported his views.

In my opinion, the pact also lacks concrete strategies to address refugee participation, spelled with a capital P, in the operationalization of the proposed policy changes. I have been in this field for over 30 years and we constantly talk about refugee participation, but hardly ever implement it in meaningful ways. Decisions about us are always made without us. The Global Refugee Forum did include 80 refugees, but the participants noted that very little of the three billion dollars pledged was going to refugee-led initiatives.

The New Pact on Asylum and Migration has been launched under the fifth priority of the European

Commission, namely 'Promoting our European Way of Life' program and is a response to the flaws in the system that have been visible during the so-called 'migration crisis.' Situating the pact within the 'European Way of Life' seems to be in line with populist notions about preserving European values—whatever that means. As an anthropologist, I am very critical of essentializing cultures and making a diverse group of countries into a monolithic unit. Moreover, some of the values promoted as European values are quintessentially democratic values and upheld by many democracies, not just in Europe.

Recently, 'European values' have been invoked both to support refugees and migrants and to attack them. On the one hand, demagogues such as Viktor Orbán have positioned themselves as defenders of a Christian Europe and enacted anti-migrant policies to protect Europe from being overrun by Muslims. On the other hand, humanitarians often appeal to a vision of Europe 'As a community of nations that has overcome war and fought totalitarianism.' It seems that both visions are wrong. Orbán's rendition omits the fact that Europe is a diverse continent, in which Christian, Muslim, Jewish, and secular traditions have been present for centuries. Orbán's vision also claims that refugees and asylum seekers present a threat to 'European' traditions of tolerance, freedom, and democracy. History reminds us that these principles have been fought for and won, usually against the violent resistance of European elites.

Ironically, many of the refugees seeking safe haven in Europe have struggled for the same values and rights in their home countries.

The vision endorsed by humanitarians presents Europe as a beacon of hope to the rest of the world. Europe is in the position to affect the world for better or worse, and pressing politicians to live up to such an ideal is certainly worthwhile. However, this aspiration will remain unfulfilled if we ignore the fact that while the nations of Europe have overcome war and fought totalitarianism, many of these same nations became rich and powerful by conquering and administering huge empires, which were partially justified by the idea of European racial supremacy.

Let's not forget the history of Europe. Let's also remember that European racism is not a thing of the past and that Europeans need continued education about racism, and skills to fight it.

As you remember, during the so-called 'migration crisis' the Polish government widely criticized the actions taken by the EU. This Polish resistance to European actions found support in the Visegrad Group (V4) which was chaired by Poland in 2016–2017. In a Joint Statement from September 16, 2016, the V4 has expressed concern about the 'decreasing sense of security among (…) citizens' and in order to improve it, backed strengthening of Frontex and improving the interoperability of the EU databases. Further, they supported cooperation with third countries to protect borders but in regards to the relocation scheme, they stated that migration policy should be based on the principle of 'flexible solidarity,' which means that member states should be able to decide about the way they want to help and do so voluntarily. Indeed, the Polish government and politicians from the ruling party have declared many times that they are ready to help but only financially.

It seems that the third floor --cooperation with third countries to protect borders—caters directly to the priorities of the conservative and anti-immigrant member states such as Hungary, Poland, and Slovakia. The pact allows members to opt out from participating in the relocation of asylum seekers and refugees within the EU by offering them the possibility to instead provide administrative and financial support to other member states. Serious doubts have been expressed about the viability of this scheme.

The Polish and Hungarian Prime Ministers, Mateusz Morawiecki and Viktor Orbán, are not convinced that the new pact will not hit their countries with a quota relocation scheme. The spokesperson for Orbán has in fact claimed that the new Pact still includes a quota but under a different name and this won't be accepted by Hungary. This objection towards a mandatory relocation system has already been voiced by the V4 (joined by Estonia, Latvia, and Slovenia) in June 2020 in their letter to European Commission Vice-President Margaritis Schinas and Commissioner Ylva Johansson. Even though the

New Pact can be seen as a step towards a compromise on the part of the European Commission, countries such as Poland and Hungary are unlikely to abandon their position, which has been so important to their electoral stance.

Challenges abound outside Europe, but perhaps this is a topic for another book and another author.

Further Reading

Richard Black, Godfried Engbersen, Marek Okólski, and Cristina Panţîru. 2010. *A Continent Moving West? EU Enlargement and Labour Migration from Central and Eastern Europe*. Amsterdam University Press.

Alice Bloch, Nando Sigona, and Roger Zetter. 2014. *Sans Papiers: The Social and Economic Lives of Young Undocumented Migrants*. Pluto Press.

Christina Boswell and Andrew Geddes. 2011. *Migration and Mobility in the European Union*. Palgrave Macmillan.

Jason De Leon and Michael Wells. 2015. *The Land of Open Graves: Living and Dying on the Migrant Trail*. California University Press.

Roberto G. Gonzales, Nando Sigona, Martha C. Franco, and Anna Papoutsi. 2019. *Undocumented Migration: Borders, Immigration Enforcement, and Belonging*. Polity Press.

Roberto G. Gonzales and Nando Sigona (eds.) 2017. *Within and Beyond Citizenship: Borders, Membership and Belonging*. Routledge.

Roberto G. Gonzales. 2016. *Lives in Limbo: Undocumented and Coming of Age in America.* California University Press.

Reece Jones. 2016. *Violent Borders. Refugees and the Right to Move.* Verso.

Shauna Labman and Geoffrey Cameron (eds.). 2020. *Strangers to Neighbours. Refugee Sponsorship in Context.* McGill-Queen's University Press.

Susan F. Martin. 2014. *International Migration. Evolving Trends from the Early Twentieth Century to the Present.* Cambridge University Press.

Susan F. Martin. 2010. *A Nation of Immigrants.* Cambridge University Press.

Susan Forbes Martin. 2003. *Refugee Women.* Second Edition. Lexington Books.

Adriana Mica, Anna Horolets, Mikołaj Pawlak, Paweł Kubicki. 2021. *Ignorance and Change. Anticipatory Knowledge and the European Refugee Crisis.* Routledge.

Fiddian-Qasmiyeh, Gil Loescher, Katy Long, and Nando Sigona. 2016. *The Oxford Handbook of Refugee and Forced Migration Studies*. Oxford University Press.

Peter Tinti and Tuesday Reitano. 2017. *Migrant, Refugee, Smuggler, Savior*. Oxford University Press.

Isabel Wilkerson. 2010. *The Warmth of Other Suns. The Epic Story of America's Great Migration*. Vintage Books.

Parts of this book are based on my own publications the readers might find of interest.

Elżbieta M. Goździak. 2021. *Human Trafficking as a New (In)Security Threat*. Palgrave Macmillan.

Elżbieta M. Goździak, Izabella Main, and Brigitte Suter (eds.) 2020. *Europe and the Refugee Response. A Crisis of Values?* Routledge.

Marie Louise Seeberg and Elżbieta M. Goździak (eds.) 2016. *Contested Childhoods: Growing Up in Migrancy*. Springer Publishing.

Elżbieta M. Goździak. 2016. *Trafficked Children and Youth in the United States: Reimagining Survivors*. Rutgers University Press.

Elżbieta M. Goździak and Susan F. Martin. 2005. *Beyond the Gateway: Immigrants in a Changing America*. Lexington Books.

Quick Immersion Series

1   **De-Extinctions,** Carles Lalueza-Fox

2   **Populisms,** Carlos de la Torre

3   **Happiness,** Amitava Krishna Dutt and Benjamin Radcliff

4   **The Science of Cooking,** Claudi Mans

5   **Aristotle,** C.D.C. Reeve

6   **Jewish Culture,** Jess Olson

7   **Fascism,** Roger Griffin

8   **Nonviolence,** Andrew Fiala

9   **The French Revolution,** Jay M. Smith

10 **Jazz,** Joel Dinerstein

11 **The Cathedral of Notre-Dame of Paris,** Kevin D. Murphy

12 **Civil Rights,** Andrew Altman

13 **Feminism,** Noëlle McAfee

14 **International Migration,** Elżbieta M. Goździak

For more information, please follow us on Facebook @TibidaboPublishing or visit www.quickimmersions.com

www.ingramcontent.com/pod-product-compliance
Lightning Source LLC
Chambersburg PA
CBHW050131280326
41933CB00010B/1329